D1327104

WOMAN POWER
IN
TEXTILE
AND
APPAREL SALES

WOMAN POWER
IN
TEXTILE
AND
APPAREL SALES

Jerry Sherman
AND
Eric Hertz

FAIRCHILD PUBLICATIONS
New York

790725

Copyright © 1979 by Fairchild Publications
Division of Capital Cities Media, Inc.

All rights reserved. No part of this book may be reproduced in
any form without permission in writing from the publisher,
except by a reviewer who wishes to quote passages in
connection with a review written for inclusion in a magazine or
newspaper.

Standard Book Number: 87005-199-7

Library of Congress Catalog Card Number: 78-61155

Printed in the United States of America

Contents

Preface

At a time when women are becoming a major factor in the national labor force, relatively few women have elected to pursue careers in sales. Although selling is perhaps the key route to advancement in many fields, women have tended to shy away from the sales arena and, in so doing, have deprived themselves of considerable opportunity for financial gain and increased management responsibility.

Particularly in the apparel and textile field, a shortage of women in key sales positions is apparent. This is a striking and ironic situation in an industry which manufactures clothing for women and is heavily populated with female designers and fashion personnel.

One explanation is that sales has always retained a "male mystique." The image of the back-slapping, threadbare traveling salesman persists in many women's minds, and they perceive selling as a rather undignified, male-oriented activity. To some extent, management has been guilty of fostering this image of the exclusive male "selling club" and has deterred ambitious women from seeking positions in the sales departments of apparel and textile companies.

Nothing could be further from the truth. Selling in today's business community is considered a highly respectable, lucrative, and professional pursuit. Because success in sales so often means advancement to top management positions within a company, women have often been cut out of the action at the top simply because they lack selling experience. The large majority of corporate executives in the apparel and textile field—presidents, vice-presidents, general managers—have emerged in recent years from the sales arena rather than from fashion, production, or finance departments.

The reason for this is simple: Selling the product is the most competitive part of the apparel and textile manufacturing and marketing process. No matter how well-designed an article of clothing may be, if the company is not successful in getting its merchandise onto department store racks and into the consumer's hands, there is no future for the business.

As professionals in the apparel industry, we feel that women represent a great untapped resource for sales and, ultimately, management posts. Having talked with a number of women who hold key sales positions in the field, we are convinced that women have as much innate sales ability as men. In fact we believe that at times women actually surpass men in their sensitivity to customer needs and their instinct for the customer's mood and willingness to buy.

As you read the chapters that follow, you are likely to be surprised by some of the women you meet. More than a few of the women in sales today are big money earners—often commanding better pay than many of the men in their companies. They are highly ambitious, putting careers on an equal footing with family life and working out ingenious schedules which enable them to juggle effectively the demands of job and home together. They are competitive and savvy in the ways of the business world and have earned the respect of their male counterparts and superiors on the sales staffs of leading companies in the apparel and textile industry.

A precious few have graduated through the sales ranks to top executive positions with major firms. They are in the vanguard of a new movement—the successful entry of women into the industry's most prestigious and responsible top management jobs.

This book is designed as a complete guide for the woman who would like to succeed in apparel and textile sales. It is useful to women who have never sold before in their lives, and who have had no firsthand experience in the fashion industry. It is equally purposeful to women who have secured jobs with textile or apparel companies, but have had difficulty moving into the sales area or gaining advancement.

Successful selling is not a mystery. Put simply, selling involves the mastery of certain basic techniques and the utilization of one's own instincts and psychology to determine customer needs and desires. In the forthcoming pages we describe these effective sales techniques and, through interviews with leading saleswomen, show you how these tools are integrated with their own personal approaches to selling.

We also illustrate some of the critical mistakes women often make in the sales field and show how these can be avoided by the trained salesperson.

We wish to thank Maggie Zander, illustrator; and Elaine Golt Gongora, book designer.

We are most grateful to our editor, Olga Kontzias, whose assistance and direction have helped immeasurably in the organization of this work.

1979   Jerry Sherman
                                                                    Eric Hertz

The Roadblocks to Success

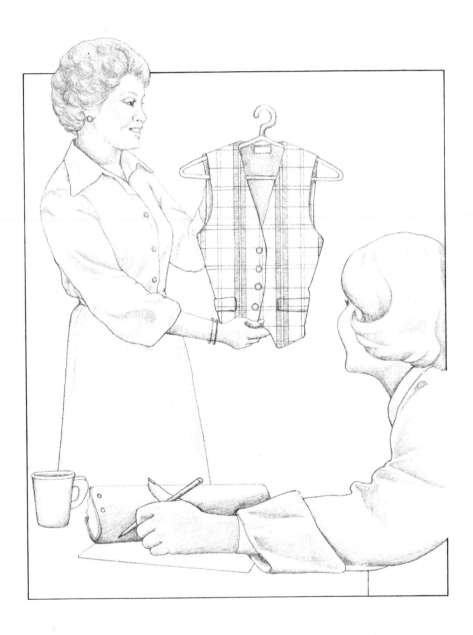

*M*arion has that striking directness—the ability to talk through you—which is the sign of a $60,000-a-year salesperson. In fact Marion worked for a year as the New York metropolitan area sales representative for a medium-sized apparel company—a job she took on salary because she felt no high-paying commission jobs were available to women. She earned $15,000 that year.

Then, suddenly, it all fell apart. The purchasing agent for a big chain-store account had taken more than a casual liking to Marion, a perky twenty-four-year old with flaxen blond hair and sharp blue eyes. She encouraged the agent's advances, which led to larger orders. But when Marion sought to secure firm working relations with a vice-president of the chain—the purchasing agent's boss—the agent got jealous. He mixed up her orders and caused lost shipments, incorrect assortments, special charges for damaged goods, and penalties for late payments.

"It was a hopeless situation," says Marion. "And word had gotten through to my boss of the screw-ups." Two weeks later Marion lost the account; the following month she was out of a job.

A former junior high school teacher, Beverly found herself in the apparel business after she was laid off by the New York City school system. She took a job selling swimsuits out of a manufacturer's showroom. Beverly, who has a master's degree in education, quickly took a liking to the fast-paced, prestige-conscious apparel business. She would have liked to get out on the road where the big commissions are made—$60,000, $80,000, $100,000, and more to top salespeople—and then perhaps take over as vice-president of sales and marketing for a large manufacturer.

Instead she spends each day selling bikinis off a rack to whomever chooses to stop by the showroom. She is getting a $10,000 flat salary, with no raises in sight. "I don't want to be a showroom girl all my life," she says. "Anyone is trainable for a showroom job. I can do more than show a line—I'm capable of thinking things through, developing a concept that will sell, and building a rapport with people.

"I don't feel that I'm contributing to this company in an important way. And I hate doing things in an unplanned manner. But I just don't know how to move out of this."

Evelyn spent two years traveling around the Poconos and northern Pennsylvania in a Chevy Nova—with two forty-piece apparel bags and a collapsible display rack in the trunk. "I liked it at first," she says. "I had to eat alone, drink alone, sleep alone. But it was a good time for a single girl—I was out and moving around all the time."

She was twenty-one when she started, with a degree in business from a two-year junior college. Considering her age and lack of experience, the $25,000 she earned each year in commissions made it all worth the effort. A good part of those commissions came from a large department store account in the Lehigh Valley. Evelyn entertained the store's merchandise manager on a regular basis—a practice which swiftly escalated from the routine lunches to dinners, movies, and nightclubs. Before she knew it, servicing the account became an all-night affair.

She was in over her head, and the account was on the block. Evelyn tried to scrape up more business from secondary accounts to make up for the pending loss. When the merchandise manager finally closed the account with her firm, she lost a third of her total commissions. Shortly after she was called back to sell out of the company's New York showroom—on a $12,000 straight salary.

The above experiences are typical of women who have entered the field of apparel and textile sales, but found themselves trapped by a combination of antifeminist bias and self-doubt. The apparel/textile field is not unique in this regard. Virtually every major American industry has been male-oriented and, until very recently, few women have dared to penetrate the ranks of sales management and move up to the executive turf which lies beyond.

But the fashion industry holds a special allure for women aspiring to business careers, and rightfully so. Fashion, after all, is in large part predicated upon the moods and desires of women. The fastest growing, most dynamic segment of the apparel industry—women's sportswear and casual apparel—is wholly dependent upon the whims and tastes of the wide-ranging female population.

So why then does the apparel-textile industry—and particularly the *women's* apparel industry—continue to be male-dominated? And why can't a bright, well-educated, highly motivated American female make a successful career as a businesswoman in the textile and apparel field?

The fact is there are dozens of successful women who have risen through the ranks of secretary, showroom sales, route salesperson, sales manager, and finally executive level positions at the top of major apparel and textile concerns. They have made it through a combination of hard-driving determination and a good sound confidence in their business know-how, as well as the hidden persuasive advantages of female charm in a male-dominated society.

These women have proved it is possible to integrate the cabalistic male society of territory salesmen—to get out on the road and earn big dollars, acquire major financial responsibilities for a company, and then move ahead to top-level management positions. They are *not* necessarily designers. But their merchandising sense enables them to hire and direct a garment or fabric designer toward concepts that can be merchandised. One female president of a women's sportswear firm even hired a *male* designer!

They have demonstrated that there is no longer a ceiling to the financial rewards women may expect—rewards which have proved bountiful to successful men in the fashion business. Some of these women are earning $80,000 to $100,000 and more a year, with lucrative stock options and other executive benefits from their corporations.

Although they are strong-willed by and large, they are certainly not Titans. Rather each of them experienced setbacks similar to those recounted by Marion, Evelyn, and Beverly. In some cases they entered the industry after years of absence—time spent raising families, doing charitable work—before finding their calling in the fashion industry.

But once having plunged into the white-water currents of a highly competitive business, each of them developed instincts for swimming upstream—for actually turning around the supposed obstacles to feminine advancement, and using these to their advantage.

In this book the successful women executives share their secrets with you and explain how they surmounted roadblocks which have kept other women back. They show you that with the right qualifications, and by following a strategy of proven effectiveness, you too can achieve considerable financial rewards and executive authority in a fast-paced, exciting industry.

You learn:

- How to secure an entry-level job with an apparel or textile company—even if you've never had any experience whatsoever.
- How to work your way quickly through the ranks and to net a top-paying job as manager of your own sales territory.

- How to play the game of corporate politics to boost your image and prestige within the company.
- How to attain the top-level management position you are seeking and to hold onto it by carrying out executive responsibilities effectively and smoothly.

The Female Sales Executive—Three Portraits

"**P**eople used to look at me and ask, 'A woman selling piece goods? Never!' " That was three years ago, when Terry Wells took a job with the Klopman apparel fabrics division of Burlington Industries, selling fabrics to the men's wear trade. She was thirty-two, mother of two strapping young kids, hankering for a stimulating career and a steady income.

And willing to work hard. "I never thought I could have so many calluses on my hands, so many blisters on my feet, at one time," she says, recalling those early months in her sales career. The first day at work Ms. Wells was harnessed with a twenty-pound bag of sample fabrics and sent on the rounds of the New York City men's wear market with a sales list "to cut my teeth on"—two dozen of the toughest accounts on the street.

"They were high-priced, designer clothing manufacturers, the type we had never really sold fabrics to before. But I saw an opportunity to build a new market for the company, to develop a foothold for us in the higher-priced end of the men's wear trade."

Ms. Wells, a personable black woman and former fashion model, took to her assignment with gusto. She quickly became popular with the designers who produce the prestige men's clothing lines, and brought in one new account after another. Three years and countless calluses later she was named sales manager of the Gotham Place division at Klopman—a division which was formed especially to handle the higher-priced men's wear accounts. She is known at this writing as one of the most successful sales talents—male or female—in the textile business.

Ms. Wells has earned the admiration of executives throughout the $3 billion Burlington textile conglomerate, the largest in the country. The current annual report of Burlington Industries prominently features her picture inside, and she is quoted—along with other Burlington executives—on its cover.

Still at the beginning of what she expects to be a long career in the textile industry, Ms. Wells is earning well over $40,000 a year, and she blithely forecasts a fifty percent pay increase over the next two years. In fact it is still hard for her to believe that just four years ago she was selling chewing gum for the Beech-Nut Company.

"I knew from the beginning that I wanted to work in sales," she says. "I wanted to be outside, moving around, not sitting behind a desk from nine to five.

"And I relished the thought of being one of the few women in a man's world. I felt I wasn't just working to build my own career, but to open the door for other women to enter a career I found challenging and highly rewarding."

A distinctive dresser, Ms. Wells preferred selling fashion fabrics to chewing gum and hard candies, and landed the sales job at Burlington in 1973. "I was one of two women who were hired at that time in the Klopman division," she says. Thanks largely to her success Klopman now has fifteen saleswomen—some of them aspiring sales executives—on its staff.

Ms. Wells feels she owes a large part of her success to Burlington's sales training program, in which she participated during her first month on the job. "They taught us not only how to sell, but how to work with people. I learned how to listen—really listen —when someone else is talking, how to pick up every nuance of a conversation. I learned when to take a soft approach to selling, and when to assume a harder tack."

What personal characteristics should the successful saleswoman have? "The number one characteristic is personality, and appearance runs a close number two. When people first meet you, they don't know your ability, so personality and appearance help get you through the door."

Being a woman is a distinct advantage in textile sales, says Ms. Wells: "It stimulates curiosity and interest in the market." But she quickly adds, "I take a strictly business approach. I handle myself in a decorous way, and I don't put up with flirtatious appeals. I told myself from the beginning that I'm in this to sell piece goods—not to be wined and dined.

"The market, which at first appears to be so large, is actually a small world. Your reputation is established very quickly—and it must be a good one."

Ms. Wells says her career outlook has never been brighter. "Not a week goes by when I don't receive an offer from another company. Today textile companies are looking specifically for women in sales positions. When you reach my stage of development, the field is wide open." However she feels she has carved out a career for herself at Burlington, and expects a promotion to divisional head and ultimately a corporate executive post.

Ms. Wells says women should not be fooled into thinking of sales as a glamorous field. "You can make money at this business —much more money than being a secretary or a teacher, jobs traditionally held by women. But it's not easy, and the glamour quickly fades when you have to go out with heavy sample bags in pouring rain or fifteen-degree weather.

"You've got to really want to sell."

"I have always seen myself as a feminist," says a top buyer at one of the nation's largest retail chains. "I wear an Equal Rights Amendment bracelet to work every day."

This buyer is one feminist who has found her place within the male-dominated retail executive arena. She buys women's coordinated sportswear—one of the store's most important apparel categories—and is confident that in time she will assume a high-level executive post with the firm which has several billion dollars in annual sales.

"I have learned through my experience with this company that it is important to do things in an evolutionary way, not a revolutionary way. Women are learning to utilize the system, rather than bucking it, to gain recognition from top management. We've learned to sell them on our ideas and influence their decisions."

The buyer wanted to pursue a career in fashion ever since she was a child, peering through fashion magazines at her family's summer home. "All the kids would go for a swim in the lake, but I would spend hours looking through the fashion books."

She sold sportswear in the campus store at college while earning a BA in English. "I learned that I was a salesperson before anything else." Once out of school she took a job selling designer clothing at Bloomingdale's in New York at the time that the store was just beginning to cement its high-fashion image. "It was a real learning experience," she recalls. "I found out how to promote your top styles on a T-stand, and mark down your dogs."

Then she dropped out of the work force to rear a family. It wasn't without misgivings. "I would read about the top women in retailing—Francine Farkas of Alexander's, Geraldine Stutz at Henri Bendel. I thought if they could do it, so could I."

When her second child was just six months old, the buyer plunged back into retailing by answering a want ad in *The New York Times*. The employer turned out to be the major national chain, and the job was assistant buyer of a new junior sportswear department.

"A lot of smaller stores had told me I couldn't hold down a job with two young kids at home. But these people gave me the go-ahead," she says. The year was 1965, the time of the great "midi" debacle in the women's fashion industry. Consumers were balking at the racks of long skirts in department stores, creating havoc in the women's apparel market.

"I could see early on that customers weren't buying the new

look. So I concentrated our stocks in other areas—building up shorter-skirt inventories and promoting blouses and sweaters." As a result the chain store's volume actually increased in the sportswear category during a declining market period. She was rewarded with full buying responsibilities in the misses sportswear area. In her current position she has helped steer the mammoth retailer into a higher-priced fashion posture in women's wear.

"Management told me they wanted to be in the fashion business. So I implemented a fashion program in the women's sportswear category, expanding better fashion looks from just a few isolated stores to over 150 branches. We're giving the customer increased quality and selling merchandise at higher prices and more profitably than in the past," she says.

This female executive feels the retail area is more responsive to women seeking top management responsibilities than in years past. But she says women still have to be on guard in a male-dominated environment. "There's a very fine line that women have to walk in this business. An aggressive woman is very threatening to her male peers and superiors, and often works against herself.

"I've come to see this as a selling job. I have to convince the men I'm working with that I'm on their side, and not trying to unseat them. I have to be aggressive—and still be a woman about it."

She says women should prepare themselves for indignities they are likely to suffer along the way. "When somebody asks me at this stage in my career if I'm serious about my work, I feel like punching them. Women are just as serious about their careers as men. I've always had a five-year plan. Believe me, it's important for a woman to define her goals and plan how to attain them—even if you don't always fulfill that plan. For the most part I've achieved my goals in business."

The buyer finds she has been able to manage the dual role of business executive and family woman. "My children have completely adjusted to my becoming a career woman. We may not have a tighter family for it, but we have a broader family than most, with a wider range of interests."

"I wasn't really looking for a job as president of a women's apparel company. I thought a chief executive in this industry would need a solid business background, and lots of management experience," says Nancy Ebker, as she leans back in the felt-covered armchair of a major women's sportswear company in New York City, overlooking the Hudson River.

Ms. Ebker, a women's sportswear designer for the past fifteen years, found herself in this top spot in late 1976. At that time management decided the dress and sportswear company needed a new fashion and merchandising direction to reestablish its position in the fast-paced women's wear market.

A one-time major force in the industry, this company had been "sliding," according to Ms. Ebker, due to the lack of a strong fashion image. "It's a challenge for me to develop a new range of customers for this company, and to regain our former strength in the department stores," she says.

"I have found that, to a large degree, business management is common sense. I already knew everything about design, merchandising, and production when I came into this job. And I've learned marketing and sales management simply by doing it."

Ms. Ebker does not fit the stereotyped image of a company president. She is tall, attractive (a former model), thirty-fivish, wears blue-tinted aviator glasses, lots of jewelry, and talks in a slow, thoughtful manner. She is candid and direct, characteristics she feels are important to women seeking top jobs in the apparel industry.

"This is a people industry," she says. "You need to share your thoughts and problems with others, be open with those around you, understand their jobs as well as your own.

"The people I've hired are not only interested in their particular assignments—whether it be sales, design, or shipping—but in all aspects of the business. I expect a shipping clerk to do cartwheels when we get a big order here in the showroom, and for our salespeople to understand the merits of good design.

"Too many people in this business are in their own little worlds. I'm trying to break down the walls, give people a feeling of togetherness." Ebker has been a generalist ever since she started designing for the Act III women's sportswear division of Jonathan Logan, a large apparel conglomerate, in 1963.

"It was a new division then, and I saw an opportunity to build. I sought autonomy—told the president of the company to let me design the first group my way, and see how it went."

She got involved in every aspect of the fledgling operation— designing, advertising, selling—and introduced a new concept: bright, colorful knit sportswear coordinates just right for the suburban American lifestyle. They were easy to wear and a snap to care for.

"In no time we built a major sportswear company," she recalls. "Our business skyrocketed to an $87 million sales level. There were at least eight companies trying to knock us off, copy us."

In her present position Ms. Ebker is gearing for another breed of customer, one which she believes is just emerging on the retail scene. "I'm looking for the younger woman who's never been in a dress before—who's spent years in jeans and pantsuits, but who is now looking for a more mature, sophisticated style of dressing."

In addition to the firm's pre-existing sportswear division, Ms. Ebker opened one of her own. The new collection features bet-ter-made sportswear for women aged twenty-eight to forty, women who can't afford expensive designer clothes, but who want a stylish, distinctive look just the same.

"There's a void in the market. Stores aren't selling this woman today," she says. "I'm working with retail management to get the concept across, and make room for it in women's sportswear departments."

According to Ms. Ebker there's virtually no limit to the money which can be earned by women apparel executives. She says she is being paid on a par with male company presidents, and that position today often brings an annual salary ranging from $80,000 to $150,000, plus bonuses and other executive benefits.

What is the major obstacle encountered by women on their way to the top? "It's important not to be afraid of acting on your ideas," says this executive. "There's so much fear—especially by women—of making a decision. By the time it should be made, it's often too late, and the results can be disastrous.

"There are an awful lot of powerful choices that have to be made in this job. I have to buy $125,000 worth of fabric before I've even seen a finished garment style."

Ms. Ebker maintains a New York City apartment where she lives with her six-year-old son. "I've been working all hours, not spending as much time with my son as I'd like to," she says. "But the time we do spend together—mostly on weekends—is valuable. I was lucky enough to find a very loving housekeeper to take care of things during the week. That's important."

What Makes a Good Sales Executive?

*Y*ou are probably wondering how one gets started in the challenging and lucrative field of apparel/textile sales. Actually, the first major step is assessing your own strengths and weaknesses frankly to determine your potential for the grinding but rewarding sales field.

GUIDELINES FOR SUCCESSFUL SELLING

Not every person is cut out for a top-notch sales position. Some people simply do not have the right combination of personal characteristics, without which a career in apparel and textile sales management would pose only frustrations, anxiety, and a lack of fulfillment.

But for those with the right chemistry, the opportunities for fulfillment and personal growth in the apparel and textile industries are almost unbounded. From the very first day on the job many of these people are hooked on the excitement of a business with a lightning pace, a roller-coaster combination of tremendous highs and alternating lows, and with an unparalleled opportunity for managerial achievement and financial reward.

What qualities must a sales professional possess? In this chapter you are provided with a barometer to measure your own potential as a sales executive—the particular skills which will prepare you for a career in the fashion industry.

Many of these characteristics may be cultivated and refined by conscientious application to on-the-job training. Even a top-notch salesperson or sales manager is constantly perfecting her technique, sharpening her sales pitch to razor-sharp accuracy, evaluating her performance in every new selling situation, refining her judgment of each client, and ascertaining that client's needs.

As you read this chapter conduct your own self-appraisal as a prospective salesperson. Make notes of your personal strengths—and also of those areas where you may feel deficient and where you may want to seek improvement during the first year or two of on-the-job work.

CONTROLLED EGO DRIVE

Do you put yourself on the line when you involve yourself in a project? Or do you maintain an objective distance from your work? When you are turned down, do you feel angered and driven to overcome the obstacle to your success? Or do you dismiss failure with a shrug of the shoulder?

The person who is angered by each victory and loss in life and motivated to overcome the source of resistance is driven by a high amount of personal self-esteem. We say he or she has a high degree of "ego drive"—the need for constant achievement and self-fulfillment.

A good salesperson is ego-driven—but in a controlled way. When she is turned down by a client she feels personally rejected. Either her sales pitch was misdirected or she was unprepared for the selling situation, unknowledgeable about the needs of her customer.

Of course, there are times when a salesperson is not wholly at fault for losing a sale. The product may be wrong for a specific client, or the customer may be a difficult and unyielding person who resists the sales presentation out-of-hand.

Whatever the obstacles to the sale, the trained salesperson doesn't allow herself to lash out at the buyer for not responding to her sales effort, destroying a relationship which has taken weeks or months to build up.

Rather she bounces back quickly from failure, realizing each sales presentation is another opportunity to restore self-confidence, to make up for past shortcomings. She is like the champion tennis player who's been badly beaten in the first set but bounces back to defeat her opponent in the next two straight sets —and to win the match. She puts the onus on herself, accepting the blame for error, gaining self-gratification from success. In fact *the remembrance of the pain of past failures is a chief motivating factor for making all future sales.*

How would you rate your own ego drive? If, after rejection, you cannot bounce back stronger and more determined to make the next sale, you may want to train yourself to have greater self-esteem—-to see yourself as someone special, with personal needs to be satisfied and advanced in the selling process.

EMPATHY

Do you often find yourself adjusting to another person's moods and behavior, modifying your own position to accommodate another viewpoint? Or do you find it difficult to anticipate the other person's actions, to accept an opinion which conflicts with your own?

The poor sales executive approaches each sale as a battle to be won at any cost. The buyer is viewed as the opponent; questions and criticisms are overruled; an attempt is made to push and bully the buyer into giving the order. To this type of salesperson the buyer—a flesh-and-blood human being with a thousand personal needs and requirements of her own—is perceived as a "big pencil," to be won over for the sake of an order, then disregarded. The "big pencil" attitude may produce a sale. But over the long run it is sure to induce hostility, mistrust, and destruction of a harmonious working relationship.

The key to successful selling is *empathy*—that rare quality which means a person understands the moods and behavior patterns of her fellow human beings, whether they are customers or peers on the sales staff. It enables the salesperson to elicit the needs of her customer, both on a business and personal level, and deal with those needs realistically. A professional salesperson adapts herself to the moods of her customers. In fact in some instances the salesperson may even find it necessary to forestall the sale and wait for a more appropriate moment.

She realizes there is no way to pre-judge the buyer's state of mind when she enters the showroom—particularly the buyer who is emotionally overwrought by personal or business problems. She doesn't fight or resist the agitated buyer, but hears her out before even attempting to sell. In this case empathy means sending up a receptive antenna and—at least temporarily—ceasing to broadcast.

Empathy also means understanding the egotistical buyer— letting him sound off, expound on his own virtues, without feeling personally eclipsed. In this case the quickest way to terminate the sale—and endanger a good working relationship—would be to preach when you are expected to be a good parishioner.

An empathetic salesperson can negotiate effectively in the turbulent waters stirred up by hostile or even hysterical buyers. She learns to participate in the buyer's anger, to assume the sense of outrage *as if it were her own,* to communicate on a high frequency, and to offer the proper corrective action which will quell the excitement and pave the way for a rational business transaction.

APPEARANCE AND COMPORTMENT

Do you dress and conduct yourself in a clean, dignified, and controlled manner? Or do you dress for maximum effect, calling attention to yourself with flashy, unconventional clothing? In this business of fashion and style, clothes are the instrument by which you make your first contact with buyer and employer alike. And the best rule is to dress naturally, if somewhat conservatively, in well-tailored, affordable clothing.

A flashy, overdressed appearance may work against you. It can signify insecurity rather than confidence in yourself and your product. In fact the big dresser is often regarded as the small businessperson whose ostentatious manner compensates for an inherent lack of talent and ability.

Don't try to win orders with a sexually alluring appearance. Your female customers will resent the "competition"; male buyers will almost certainly be distracted from the business at hand.

As a general rule of thumb *match your appearance to the product you are selling.* If you are marketing better-priced, well-tailored sportswear, your own dress should conform with this taste level. Likewise, salespeople in the moderate or budget-priced field often prefer to wear better-made clothing to exhibit their personal sense of good taste.

If your product is blue jeans and T-shirts you may find it more acceptable to dress casually. Wearing a well-tailored denim jacket-and-jeans outfit will enhance the image of your product line and gain credibility. One sales manager for a junior sweater firm dresses daily in crew-neck shetland sweaters, corduroy jeans, and saddle oxfords exhibiting a collegiate image which supports the wearability of his merchandise.

Generally speaking, sales executives with large textile companies dress more conservatively. These larger companies have established corporate identities and expect their people to conform with a prevailing mode of dress rather than buck the rules.

Likewise retail executives are also likely to conform to the image of their particular stores; generally they dress in a more conservative manner than their counterparts in the apparel industry.

An exception to these common modes of dressing is the West Coast sales executive who, due to the balmy climate and relaxed lifestyle, is apt to dress without formality. But even so the standards call for well-made, clean-looking clothing—definitely not the ragged and worn-out 60s youth style.

INWARD AGGRESSIVENESS

Beware the hot-shot salesperson; she cares not what she sells. The trick to effective, aggressive selling is *not to seem aggressive.* Never let that customer know how hungry you are to make the sale; don't let the dollar signs show through.

Every good salesperson feels an inward sense of aggressiveness which, along with fear of failure, acts as a prime motivating force. In fact aggressiveness is almost synonymous with the sales process —the need to drum up the maximum amount of business which can be properly handled by the company's manufacturing and distribution set-up.

But *don't oversell.* Once your customer has agreed to a purchase, don't try to push additional merchandise which he doesn't want or can't possibly handle. If you've tried to contact the buyer by phone without success, don't leave a pile of messages with his secretary—it's a real turn-off. If a buyer cannot be reached, don't automatically go over his or her head to the merchandise manager or other store executive. You will have earned an enemy in that buyer.

Aggressive behavior, properly employed, is really creative behavior—finding a way to maneuver a seemingly impossible situation into a sale. Take that aloof, unresponsive buyer who won't pay a visit or return a call. Don't give up. The key to contacting him may rest with a friendly assistant buyer, or a conscientious secretary who, once cultivated, can make the contact for you. Such an intermediary can communicate your message to the buyer—and frequently ascertain the buyer's reaction. He or she becomes, in a sense, an extension of your sales staff, assisting and nurturing the sale.

Sometimes locating a friend of the buyer in the marketplace or at the store will help you establish a *center of influence* from which to contact him. More often than not if you approach people in a friendly manner, you will find them interested in your problem and willing to do a favor.

These are just a few examples of how aggressiveness can be translated into resourceful channels by effective salespeople.

INTEGRITY

We have all heard "integrity," from our scouting days onward, preached as some vague moralistic code by which we should abide. But for the sales executive integrity carries a very special meaning. It defines one's character and reputation in the market-place, forms the backbone of that person's credibility, and is a major factor in gaining the trust and admiration of superiors in the company and clients alike.

What is integrity in the business world? It is, simply, *describing things as they are and making commitments stand.* What you say is what you do—or you don't say it. You are judged primarily on your performance; your accomplishments must live up to your promises.

A lot of inferior salespeople make promises which they can't possibly fulfill, resulting in frequent chaotic situations: undelivered orders, late shipments, overproduction of mer-chandise which they've ordered but can't sell. They are con-stantly backing and filling, making excuses, covering them-selves up against impending disaster. For this reason it's the salesperson who lives up to her promises who gains immense respect.

The salesperson with integrity operates on a realistic basis. If a store calls to complain of a late shipment, she promises immedi-ate action rather than procrastinating. When it is found the shipment has been lost in the manufacturer's warehouse, the salesperson tells the buyer the truth—not that there's been a work slowdown, or a truck was lost en route, or the store's stock-room must have misplaced the merchandise.

Or suppose, for example, a buyer calls demanding ship-ment in three days, when you know it will take at least three weeks. Integrity means you tell that buyer the truth—whether or not you lose the order as a result. You won't lose the account!

In short integrity makes you unique in the selling environment. Even if your buyers or your peers don't have it, it is incumbent upon you to possess it.

CREATIVITY

Do you tend to follow instructions in an unquestioning manner, accepting a course of action because "that's the way we've always done it?" Or do you perceive the way a situation is being handled, then ask yourself, "How can I do it better?"

Creativity in sales means taking a thorough look at the existing sales practices of your company, then translating them into your own course of action. It means imposing your own style on the sales relationship and winning recognition for changes and improvements which you have instituted.

Many salespeople simply act as conduits between the manufacturing plant and the retailer. They honor their commitments on time. But they fail to inject their own personal style into the transaction—to guide the buyer into the best possible merchandise selections for his store, or to offer advice on how best to display and stock specific styles.

There's a new and growing style of selling which every aspiring sales executive should know and adopt: It involves working closely with the stores to develop creative methods of merchandising, ensuring the "sell-through" of the company's product line to retail customers. No longer is it acceptable to simply "sell and be done with it," leaving the buyer to struggle with merchandising and display problems on his own.

Similarly the creative textile salesperson understands that the selling process is never complete until the goods are moving out of the customer's—apparel manufacturer's—showroom. Developing tools for merchandising the finished clothing, and for communicating color, style, and fabric directions which help the sale of the finished product are the responsibility of the contemporary textile sales executive.

EMOTIONAL MATURITY

Do you get carried away with your emotions under stress or in the throes of a difficult decision? Or are you able to accept strain and conflict as a normal part of your working day? The buying and selling process is an emotional one. Decisions are made involving tens and hundreds of thousands of dollars worth of merchandise. Buyers are frequently, and understandably, insecure about spending the large sums of money which are allotted to them for stocking their retail departments.

The ability not to lose your cool under pressure, even when the customer is emotionally high pitched or noticeably insecure, is an essential characteristic of a good salesperson. Always stay in control, realizing that if you maintain your composure you will exert a reassuring influence on your customers and nudge them toward an affirmative decision.

A SIMPLE TEST FOR SALES ABILITY

How do you rate against other practicing and prospective salespeople in your possession of the necessary selling characteristics? The short test that follows has been devised by the sales manager of a large apparel company to identify the qualifications of candidates for sales positions in his company. By rating yourself honestly on each of the criteria discussed in this chapter, you will gain an awareness of how you compare with practicing salespeople in the industry. In short you will know whether a position in apparel and textile sales is right for you.

To the right of each characteristic place a number which you feel best reflects the degree to which you possess each of these characteristics. Use the following scale:

5—possess to an extreme degree
4—possess to own satisfaction
3—possess to some extent
2—possess an insufficient amount
1—don't possess at all

1. Ego Drive— $(\times 4) =$ 4
2. Empathy— $(\times 4) =$ 5
3. Appearance— $(\times 1) =$ 5
4. Aggressiveness— $(\times 5) =$ 4
5. Integrity— $(\times 3) =$ 4
6. Creativity— $(\times 2) =$ 4
7. Emotional Maturity— $(\times 1) =$ 5

Total: _____

To determine your score: (1) Multiply your rating for each characteristic by the weighing factor alongside it in parentheses; (2) add the resulting products to obtain your total score.

Apply the following ratings to your score:

90–100 = excellent sales potential
80–90 = good sales potential; some improvement needed
70–80 = satisfactory potential; need considerable improvement through practice
Under 70 = does not show adequate potential; great amount of work will be needed to master the selling process

How to Get the Job That's Right for You

"**A**ll right," you may say. "You've sold me. Apparel and textile sales is a highly rewarding field, remarkably lucrative, high on personal gratification, and a sure road to management and corporate responsibility. But where do I fit in? How can I, with little or no experience in this specialized field, land a starting job that will lead to a successful and self-fulfilling career?"

If you're in school or college you may be afraid of stepping out into that great, uncharted expanse known as the "job market," or of taking a spin on the roulette wheel of employment opportunities. If you're a housewife with many years of childrearing experience, you may wonder whether you have skills and characteristics which are salable to a prospective employer—if, in fact, you are a desirable job candidate.

If you're already working at a job you consider too limiting in terms of responsibility and pay, you may be rationalizing your current situation in terms of the vacations, security, and petty benefits you are receiving—afraid to venture out into a new, more risky environment, where the rewards are more satisfying and the opportunities far greater. Or you simply may not know how to approach a job change.

We're not going to mislead you into believing a career in apparel, textile, and retail sales and management is easy, buffeted with a protective coating of safe decisions, painless efforts, and relaxed comfort. As you can judge from the personal accounts of the women in Chapter Two, it involves hard work, a fair amount of stress—both physical and emotional wear-and-tear—and little certainty. There is also considerable frustration along the way.

But most women who choose such a career find the rewards are well worth the effort. A surprising number of women who start out as salespeople in apparel and textile companies—and sales clerks in department stores—rise through the ranks to positions of importance as sales managers, merchandise managers, and—more and more frequently—corporate executives.

Locating a job as a salesperson in this industry is not nearly as difficult as it may seem. However there are certain proven methods you should adopt in launching and carrying out your job campaign.

JOB HUNTING: GETTING GEARED UP

The hardest part of any job campaign is the very beginning: Developing the momentum which will carry you into the employment process, through the applications and job interviews, and deposit you in the sales department of a manufacturing firm or in the selling operation of a retail chain.

The first thing you'll need to set the wheels of the employment process in motion is *self-assurance.* Remember: The odds are very much in your favor. No matter how long the job-seeking process may take—whether it be several days, weeks, or months—there are more sales jobs available than there are competent, promising talented people to fill them.

Sales is a volatile business. Most sales managers in the apparel and textile industry would like to latch onto a good prospect once she appears. The value of any sales operation is measured not in terms of the number of salespeople it involves, but in the productivity of each person.

The opportunities to gain employment in sales are greater than in other areas of business for two reasons:

1. There is a higher turnover of sales personnel. Successful salespeople move up quickly into the corporate ranks or out to a better opportunity with another firm. There is also frequent underperformance by salespeople who are not qualified for their positions, and who must be replaced.

2. Hiring in sales usually takes precedence over any other division of a company, because the dollar intake from the sales
   department is the lifeblood for all company operations.

In short the more productive salespeople a company hires, the
more profitable and powerful it becomes.

As a woman you have certain distinct advantages in a selling
situation—advantages which should serve as a source of confidence during the job hunt.

According to David King, president of Careers for Women,
Inc., a sales training and recruitment firm in New York City,
"The old standard sales formula of male aggressiveness and intimidation doesn't apply anymore. The customer doesn't want to be
pushed around. The time is right for a warmer, more easy-going
sales approach—one to which women are usually very well-suited.

"Women can be very disarming, casual, honest, and effective
in the new style of selling, which involves concern for the client's
needs and careful explanation and understanding of the product's
benefits," King adds.

This new, more sophisticated approach to sales is called *consultative selling.* As one apparel sales manager describes it, "We sit
on the same side of the table with the buyer and talk about
market conditions and business in general—not just about selling
one garment style. We act as friends and advisors, rather than
hard-nosed salespeople. But, of course, we don't for a minute lose
sight of the objective—negotiating the best possible sales
arrangement."

In the consultative selling approach, says King, saleswomen
often enjoy more rapport with their customers because they are
not trapped in the hard-sell mold, and they relate to the customer
more naturally on a personal level.

"One saleswoman whom I accompanied to a sales presentation was a great jogger," he recalls. "The product manager
she was trying to sell had a book about running on his desk,
and the two of them engaged in a delightful discussion about
where to run in New York City. In half an hour she wrapped

up one of the biggest sales contracts her company had ever received."

It is this ability to establish a common interest between both parties in the selling process which ensures a harmonious relationship.

In addition to their natural sales talents, says King, many women can benefit from the federal government's Equal Employment Office in gaining the first crack at job openings. The EEO specifies that any company doing sales of more than $50,000 a year with the federal government and with a minimum of fifty employees is subject to an EEO order requiring them to hire a specified number of women and other work-force minorities over a period of time.

At first glance this regulation would seem to have little bearing on the consumer-oriented apparel industry. However, many of the large apparel and textile companies do a substantial volume of business with the armed forces—supplying clothing and fabrics for the post exchanges and for military uniforms. Therefore these companies are subject to the EEO's employment code.

Although this fact is little-known by most women entering the apparel-textile job market, it often gives them an added plus in seeking a job with a larger company. In many cases employers attempt to fill job openings with capable women before they review applications from male candidates to meet the EEO's requirements.

GETTING YOUR FOOT IN THE DOOR
There are four basic approaches to lining up a job interview: (1) Through the recommendation of "people of influence"; (2) by responding to a classified advertisement in the help-wanted pages of a newspaper; (3) prospecting for job opportunities by making "cold calls" (actually calling on companies for job interviews without advance notice), or calling ahead for interview appointments; and (4) working through an employment agency.

Using People of Influence

The surest way to line up a job interview is to seek the advice and assistance of a friend or associate who is employed in the industry. Most people are gratified to help a friend in a small way, by introducing you to the person in charge of hiring in their firm, steering you toward another opportunity in the market, or even arranging an appointment for you. If you don't know anyone in the industry, contact a friend or acquaintance who does know people in the business.

Another way of establishing contacts with influential people is by enrolling in a course of study in an evening session at a fashion school. Invariably these schools attract people from the industry, and it is easy to establish contacts in the informal, social atmosphere of the classroom.

Once you have engaged a person of influence to help in your job hunt, don't overwork that person. After the interview appointment has been set up, be prepared to do your own self-selling job. Unless it is offered, don't ask this person to "pull strings" to help secure the position you want. Most people take offense at a request of this type and regard it as going "beyond the call of duty."

Furthermore you can retain the counsel and assistance of your influential contacts throughout your job hunt if you are casual and appreciative rather than pushy and burdensome. In fact it is a good idea to express your appreciation by sending thank-you notes to both the person of influence and the interviewer you, shortly after the interview has taken place.

Using the Help-Wanted Listings

If you don't have a friend in the business, your best approach to job hunting is by responding to classified ads in the help-wanted columns of a newspaper. The best, most reliable sources for help-wanted ads in apparel-textile manufacturing and retailing on a national basis appear in _The New York Times_ (especially in the Sunday edition), and in _Women's Wear Daily_ and _Daily News_

Record, two of the most respected and widely read publications in the women's and men's apparel-textile-retail industries. *WWD* and *DNR* are particularly helpful, since they report sales opportunities on a regional basis across the United States and are broadly distributed around the country.

The classified ads should be read carefully, since each ad tells you several important things about the prospective employer:

1. That he is eager to find the right employee quickly and therefore lists a phone number or address for immediate direct response.
2. That he is not in a great hurry and has the newspaper forward responses addressed to a box number.
3. That he has placed the ad through an outside employment agency, which is screening applicants on behalf of the employer. Note: Some agency ads represent listings they have been carrying in their files for weeks, or even months, before the job is filled. In such a case you may be one of literally hundreds of applicants being screened for the job, so the likelihood of getting the job may be small. Be wary of such repeating ads.
4. That by the adjectives and wording used in the ad, the employer is trying to find a person with certain qualities and types of experience.

You should match yourself, generally speaking, against the employer's description of the prospective salesperson ("aggressive, hard-driving" or "friendly, good people-relationships"). But don't be put off by heavy experience prerequisites or requirements like "only top-notch people need apply." The employer is often having just as hard a time as you are lining up the right contact—and frequently exaggerates for effect.

Prospecting for a Job
You don't have to wait for the right job opening to appear in the help-wanted pages to launch your own job campaign. All you need is access to a telephone, an appointment book, and a com-

fortable pair of shoes and you can form your own miniature "self-employment agency."

There are two different approaches to job prospecting: (1) making a "cold call," or unannounced visit to the employer, or (2) phoning ahead for an appointment to see the personnel director or the individual in charge of hiring. Either one, or a combination of both these techniques, can be instrumental in obtaining a job.

A surprising number of job opportunities await the ambitious prospect who happens to call on a sales manager or personnel director "cold" at the right time. The objectives of the cold call are as follows:

- To get a resume or application form on file with the employer for reference whenever a job opens up.
- To obtain an interview on the spot with a company official or to arrange an appointment at a future date.
- To gain exposure to the major apparel and textile companies in the market and to gauge the types of opportunities which are available.

Calvin Michaels, director of personnel administration for Burlington Industries, says, "If the person has the right abilities and characteristics, she can get a job in this industry simply by calling on the person in charge of hiring." He notes that among the qualities that Burlington looks for in job applicants is "high priority given to the requirements of the job—a willingness to go service the account." Initiative and drive are essentials. Therefore calling on the prospective employer exhibits the aggressiveness and motivation which are assets of a good salesperson.

Phoning ahead for a job interview can save you time and legwork, and it enables you to determine in advance the individual responsible for hiring at each company. It also gives you the opportunity to learn some things about the company before the interview, so that you can be more knowledgeable about the firm and its products when you do call for an interview. You can screen out in advance those companies which say they are "not hiring," from those which have "possible openings" or actual availabilities.

How can you locate the major employers in the apparel and textile industry to begin your "self-employment service?" Major apparel centers around the country—in New York, Los Angeles, Dallas, Chicago, Atlanta, and elsewhere—feature apparel-mart buildings, where most of the leading manufacturers are clustered together. In New York most of the manufacturers occupy showrooms in the Midtown area, along Broadway and Seventh Avenue between 34th Street and 42d Street. In the other cities there are apparel-mart centers, where virtually all manufacturers are represented in a single building complex.

Many apparel-mart buildings publish *directories* listing all the manufacturers—by apparel or textile category—in the building, with their phone numbers. These directories can be invaluable reference tools for your job hunt and can help you plan telephone calls and personal visits in a convenient manner.

In addition several trade publications in the apparel and textile field publish market directories providing detailed breakdowns of manufacturers by product category. Here are some of the best-known:

> *Women's Wear Daily* (Fairchild Publications)—publishes regular directories of the New York apparel market.
>
> *Men's Wear Magazine* (Fairchild Publications)—publishes annual directory of the men's and boys' wear market, including a list of trade associations and other helpful sources of information.
>
> *Earnshaw's Infants', Girls', Boys' Wear Review* (Earnshaw Publications Inc.)—publishes monthly directory of the children's apparel market.

In addition the following reference works are helpful guides. They can be located in many fashion school libraries and may be on file in your public library:

The Buyer's Guide, 1440 Broadway, New York City (212-354-5480)—publishes directories of the apparel and textile manufacturing markets.

Davison's Textile Blue Book, Davison's Publishing Co., Ridgewood, New Jersey (201-445-3135)—a directory of textile manufacturers and related businesses such as printing and finishing of fabrics, by geographical location.

The Salesman's Guide, 1140 Broadway, New York City (212-684-2985)—a directory of department and specialty stores and their personnel, by geographical location.

Employment Agencies

Employment agencies, especially those which emphasize job opportunities in the textile-apparel-retail industry, can be useful tools in obtaining a job. In addition there is a new species of personnel agency which specializes in jobs for women. These agencies provide women with both professional job-matching services and the ego boost which comes from meeting and working with other women who are also seeking to launch a career or advance themselves in business.

Here are some of the "new breed" of agencies and job-training centers which concentrate on female job applicants. We are not recommending or endorsing any one of these, but rather offering them for your consideration:

1. The Sales Manpower Foundation
   (A service of the Sales Executives Club)
   122 East 42nd Street
   New York, New York 10017
   (212) 661-4610
   Specialties: Clearing house for resumes, maintains file of resumes; and sends out to employers upon request.

2. Careers for Women, Inc.
   26 East 11th Street
   New York, New York 10013
   (212) 254-2192
   Specialties: Sales and marketing training courses offered; job placements secured for "graduates" of courses; job-seeking skills, including interviewing and resume preparation, are covered in the course work.

3. Fem Management Consultants, Inc.
   515 Madison Avenue
   New York, New York 10022
   (212) 759-2120
   Specialties: Consultation offered to prepare women for job market, placement services.

4. Womanschool
   170 East 70th Street
   New York, New York 10021
   (212) 688-4606
   Specialties: Training courses for women in job-finding, planning a "second career," moving out of a dead-end job, and the art of selling. Job preparation skills—including interviewing and resume-writing—are covered. "Self-marketing" in the job process is stressed.
   Additional courses offered on the campus of The College of

5. NOW (National Organization for Women)
   New York Chapter
   Career Counseling Service
   84 Fifth Avenue
   New York, New York 10011
   (212) 989-7230

Specialties: Counseling, resource and referral for careers in sales.

6. Programs in Management for Women
   Adelphi University–School of Business Administration
   Garden City, Long Island, New York 11530
   (516) 294-8700
   Specialties: Job placement service for women; conferences on management skills, communications in a business organization; Certificate Program in business administration.

If you are seeking a position in the apparel and textile field in the New York area, you should be sure to contact:

> New York State Department of Labor
> Manpower Services Division
> Apparel Industries Employment Office
> 238 West 35th Street
> New York, New York 10001
> (212) 736-1700

It is becoming more and more common for employment agencies to charge fees to the employer, rather than the job applicant. However before you accept a job from an agency, be sure to ask whether you or the employer will be paying for the service.

In addition to the agencies and training centers listed above there are several large employment agencies operating on a regional and national basis which specialize in jobs in the textile, apparel, and retail sectors. You can locate these agencies in the classified advertising section of *The New York Times, Women's Wear Daily, Daily News Record,* or most other large metropolitan daily newspapers.

Sample Resume

Marion Dale Smith
1310 Lexington Avenue
New York, New York 10016
(212) 762-8140

Summary of Background

Buyer of missy and junior moderate to better sportswear for a retail specialty store chain.

Buyer of all missy and junior budget- and popular-priced sportswear for a resident buying office.

Department manager and credit manager for a large retail operation.

Assistant buyer of accessories for a resident buying office.

Salesperson in jewelry, sportswear, and lingerie departments for a major retail store.

Skills

Experienced in all aspects of sportswear buying and merchandising including marketing, writing reports, and calculating open-to-buy. Ran a department for a large retail store; responsibilities included: inventory control, distribution of merchandise, and supervision of sales personnel.

Positions Held

1977 to Present: Buyer (sportswear)—Jones Stores, 850 Hempstead Avenue,
                       New York City

1977   : Merchandising Assistant—The Closet, Mission Boulevard,
                       Los Angeles, California

1972 to 1977   : Buyer (sportswear)—Convenient Buying Service, 500 Fifth Avenue,
                       New York City

1972   : Assistant Buyer (accessories)—Convenient Buying Service,
                       500 Fifth Avenue, New York City

1971 to 1972   : Department Manager (sportswear)—Brown's Department Store,
                       Lake Mall, Lake Success, New York

1968 to 1971   : Sales—Mindell's Department Store, Philadelphia, Pennsylvania
                       Summer and Christmas throughout college

Educational Background

Drexel University, Philadelphia, Pennsylvania—B.S. Major in Merchandising. Minor in Education.

New School of Social Research, New York City—Related courses in merchandising and the arts.

MAKING THE INTERVIEW WORK

Once you've got an interview lined up, it is important to prepare yourself in advance rather than talking off the top of your head.

Prepare a Resourceful Resume in Advance

Put yourself in the employer's shoes. If he's placed an ad in a large newspaper, he's bound to have scores, even hundreds, of responses—one looking much like the next. In preparing your resume you'll want to make it stand out, both in form and content.

"We advise women to make their resumes look different," says David King of Careers for Women. "It can be as simple as using a different color paper, or silk-screening your face right onto the page. People aren't hired on their backgrounds alone. It's important to portray yourself as an interesting person, outgoing and easy to get along with."

Some other tips:

- Don't use the same resume for every interview. Vary the content to highlight experiences and training you feel will be important to the particular employer you're visiting.
- If your experience in sales is limited, demonstrate how other jobs or life experiences have helped prepare you for a career in sales. For example, a teacher may want to indicate her ability to "sell" other staff members on her programs; a housewife who has done charitable work could mention how her efforts in soliciting funds or canvassing for support demonstrate knowledge of salesmanship techniques.
- Apparel, textile, and retail executives are often intensely busy and frequently distracted by interruptions. Make your resume brief—no longer than a page—and easy to read.

Humor the Interviewer

The most important part of a job interview is gaining rapport with the interviewer—someone you probably don't know at all.

To a large extent your success depends on the employer's opinion of you as an individual—whether you're likable, honest, industrious, a "self-starter," and a good mixer; or hostile, evasive, negligent, a "plodder," and a loner.

According to King, "The person who gets the job is the one who says what the interviewer wants her to say, and fulfills the interviewer's expectations. It's not only a matter of qualifying, but of being the preferred candidate out of many—for whatever reason."

It is important to listen very carefully and try to perceive what the interviewer is looking for in the prospective employee. Make sure your questions are intelligent and to the point, and that your answers are direct rather than evasive.

Follow-up after the Interview: Did You Get the Job?
Most of the people who are successful in obtaining jobs are those who follow through after the interview. Here are a few suggestions:

1. Get a note off to the interviewer thanking him for his time, and stating that you look forward to hearing from him shortly.
2. If you have received no response after several days, a phone call to the interviewer is in order. You may want to mention a point or two which you overlooked during the interview.
3. If the employer still shows no response, then you may want to arrange another appointment with him to discuss additional questions you have concerning the job.

The important thing is to maintain communication with the employer after the interview, right up until you receive a definitive response from the employer. This, in itself, will single you out from the scores of applicants who leave the interviewer with nothing but a faceless resume and some notes he may have taken.

LANDING A JOB IN RETAILING: A DIFFERENT APPROACH

The retail job market is much more accessible to the inexperienced job applicant than the textile or apparel manufacturing fields. To those who are qualified for an entry-level job in retail on-the-floor sales work, there are many opportunities to meet with the employer and secure a starting position.

Here's how it works. Each retail store has its own personnel office. All you need do is phone in advance to find out when interviews are being held, then go down to the store for an interview and to complete an application form. Since there is a high rate of turnover in retail sales work, opportunities for starting jobs are abundant; most likely you can find one in a store which is conveniently located near your home.

If your objective is to move swiftly into a buying job or other management post, your best bet is to apply for an executive training course within the store. If you are inexperienced at retailing, it will certainly be worth your while to grapple with the nuts-and-bolts reality of on-the-floor selling first, moving into an executive training course when the opportunity arises.

"It all depends on what stage of the game you're at," says Terry Siegel, a vice-president and merchandise manager at Macy's, New York. "If you're fifteen or sixteen and still in school, take a part-time job as a sales girl. If you have graduated from college, then jump right into a training program with a store."

Either way, prior study in retailing is not necessary, according to Ms. Siegel. "It's more important for you to be a well-rounded person than to take courses in retailing," she says. "I am impressed with a buyer who is a member of the Metropolitan Museum of Art or is a theater-goer.

"You can't really learn this business in school," she notes. "Ninety-nine percent of retailing is common sense. You can be a straight-A student in college and fall flat on your face in the retail world."

Siegel herself began her retail career in an executive training program, where she "learned about clothes" and developed an unfailing memory for brands, prices, and fabric types. She and other retailers agree the job opportunities for women are abundant in major department store chains, where men are often outnumbered by women in the top apparel buying positions.

She says, "The best job in this business is the buyer's job. You control your department, and it gives you a marvelous sense of freedom. The department, whether it be women's sportswear or men's coats, becomes a reflection of your own personality and lifestyle."

There's also a lot of exciting travel tied in with many apparel buying positions. Department store buyers commonly make frequent buying trips to Europe, where designer collections are shown in the major cities, and to the Orient, where special purchases of volume merchandise are made. Frequently top buyers make a complete circuit of the globe to satisfy their customers' demand for unusual and high-fashion clothing.

Once an aspiring executive has served as a salesperson, or graduated from a store training program, he or she will usually follow a set pattern of advances:

- *Department Manager*—responsibility for maintaining stock and display procedures in a specific department.
- *Assistant Buyer*—a post which involves all-around exposure to the buyer's responsibilities, including fiscal management, merchandise selection and timing, and advertising and sales promotion.
- *Group Manager for a Branch Store*—the supervision of several related departments in a branch unit of the chain. For example, sportswear, dresses, and beachwear are often considered a "group" of related apparel departments under a single group manager.
- *Buyer*—top responsibility for maintaining profits in a given retail department or throughout a chain of stores.

In a later chapter we discuss upper-management retail positions to which buyers can expect to graduate after years of experience and with the proper talent and expertise.

Getting Paid—How the Compensation Systems Work

*O*nce you've decided to take that promising sales job, don't be fooled into believing your compensation is determined by iron-clad rules. One of the great variables in today's job market is the paycheck. Many companies hire people at similar—sometimes identical—positions, and yet pay one quite a bit more than the other.

You play an important factor in the determination of your own pay level. A lot depends on how you impress the employer as a potential sales professional. If the employer feels he is hiring a person with a great deal of promise at his company, he is likely to offer more generous compensation than he would to a fledgling who is "here today, gone tomorrow."

You should impress the employer with your seriousness about a career in sales and your ambition to maximize your sales efforts and contributions to his business. Appear genuinely interested in the success of his particular firm, and show your commitment to its future.

Of course the best way to approach the inevitable discussion of your paycheck is to come armed with the facts on pay levels and compensation systems in the apparel and textile industry. You should strive to actively *negotiate* your compensation, rather than accept what is doled out by the employer. To do this you need to have a basic knowledge of how compensation levels are calculated, the alternative compensation plans in the industry, and how each works to the benefit of the salesperson and the employer.

In this chapter we outline the various pay systems currently in use, and the benefits and drawbacks to each. The remuneration of a *sales trainee,* or entry-level position on the sales force of a textile or apparel firm, will be quite different from that of a full-fledged *salesperson,* so we have treated each of these areas separately.

SALES TRAINEE

Many large textile companies, and a few major apparel manufacturers, take on beginners in their sales departments as trainees. The idea is to give the inexperienced person a "trial run" at sales work, under close supervision by the sales manager and with the assistance of other members of the sales force.

Unlike other sales positions the job of sales trainee is almost always a *straight salaried* position. There are rarely any bonuses, commissions, or other "incentive" pay plans attached to this salary, since the trainee does not have the experience necessary to generate substantial amounts of business for the firm.

Starting salaries for sales trainees run generally from $6,000 to $9,000 per year. The training period can run from three months to a year, after which time the trainee is either accepted as a full member of the sales force or must leave and seek a sales post elsewhere. Either way the traineeship is an invaluable tool for beginners in learning the ropes and gaining experience for future job opportunities.

Typical responsibilities of the trainee include many areas which are removed from the actual sales process, but which offer well-rounded experience in the different facets of the business. For example:

- Preparing salesmen's samples and organizing "sample bags."
- Calculating each day's sales figures and other clerical assignments.
- Carrying samples to retail stores and buying offices.
- Processing orders and assisting in the billing and shipping departments.
- Accompanying a salesman on his calls or assisting the sales manager in the office.

In short you will be asked to perform any function that is required either in the sales department or other company operations. A sales traineeship can be difficult, lackluster, and at times demeaning (sales trainees frequently perform such mundane chores as brewing the coffee and hanging the samples). However it is an invaluable source of experience. For, in today's job market, *the biggest obstacle to employment is lack of experience.* After several months as a trainee you can re-approach the job market with the great advantage of being a trained salesperson.

In accepting a position as a sales trainee make sure the training period is clearly defined. If possible get an idea of the type of accounts you will be handling. Are some of these established accounts which the company has already been selling? Or are you being given a list of rough prospects to "cut your teeth on?"

Beware the "endless training program." Six months to a year is all that's needed to break you into the field; any longer and the company is probably taking advantage of your beginner's enthusiasm and pay level while delegating to you the work of a full salesperson.

It is wise to investigate the company's sales training program before accepting a post. Is the firm serious about grooming salespeople for its own staff? Or is management interested in hiring large numbers of trainees at low pay levels to prospect for new accounts? You can easily determine this information by chatting with some of the company's sales trainees or picking up clues from competitors or customers in the industry.

Most companies require a high school degree and prefer college graduates for traineeships. A two-year college degree with a major in business can be a strong plus.

THE SALESPERSON

The large majority of apparel firms, and most of the smaller textile companies, do not have formal sales training programs. Nevertheless they hire inexperienced salespeople to be trained on the job while assisting in the sales department.

Most likely your first job will be as an "inside" salesperson responsible for generating business in the company's showroom, either through prearranged appointments with buyers or the frequent "drop-ins." You will also be required to assist other salespeople or the sales manager.

The same rule holds true of entry-level showroom sales work as of traineeship programs: Don't overstay the job. After a year you probably have all the tools necessary to advance to a full-scale sales post either inside or outside the showroom. If you can't move up within the company, don't be afraid to move out to another firm where the opportunity is greater.

Showroom salespeople are almost always *salaried,* and the average starting pay level is roughly equivalent to that of the trainee with a larger company. However in some cases showroom salespeople are paid an end-of-the-year bonus for outstanding performance, or a small add-on "commission."

The *commission* is the heart of virtually all pay systems for *outside* salespeople—those responsible for maintaining, building, and adding accounts within a given geographical area or with a given account list. By definition a commission is a form of compensation based upon percentage of the sales volume transacted by the salesperson. It is a form of "incentive" compensation: The more the person sells, the more he or she earns.

Because they are commissioned most outside sales jobs pay a higher rate of compensation than the inside positions. But the risks are far greater on the outside, and many salespeople choose to make their careers in showroom selling which offers many advantages of its own. For example:

- There is minimal travel, as opposed to the "road life" of the outside salesperson covering a regional territory.
- Inside salespeople are more accessible to management and in a better position to learn the operations of a particular firm.
- The showroom salesperson is in close communication with the company's design and merchandising staff and profits

from a good working knowledge of the design concepts which go into the product, whether it be apparel or textiles.

"OUTSIDE" OR TERRITORIAL SELLING _____

A major part of a company's sales effort is carried on outside the showroom, in the "field." In the apparel industry it is outside the office—in the executive suites of department stores or in the "back rooms" of smaller specialty stores—that many of the biggest sales are transacted. In the textile field many of the major transactions occur in the customer's (apparel manufacturer's) office.

Outside selling is the heart of the apparel and textile sales field. It involves three separate types of work:

1. *Maintaining* the company's existing accounts—particularly its larger ones—and preventing the competition from taking away important sources of business.
2. *Building* sales levels with these existing accounts, thus increasing the company's sales volume and importance in the marketplace.
3. *Opening* new accounts with customers that are not currently doing business with the firm or in areas of the country where the company's merchandise has not been sold.

Most companies delegate outside sales responsibilities only to trained salespeople; thus it is necessary to have some experience as a trainee or showroom salesperson before seeking an outside sales job.

Many outside sales jobs offer commission pay scales—but with different options. The most common arrangements are:

1. *Straight commission*—a compensation plan which pays you a direct percentage of your net shipping volume.
2. *Draw against commission*—this arrangement provides you with a regular (weekly, monthly, or bimonthly) payment which is deducted from your monthly commissions.
3. *Salary plus commission*—you are paid a weekly salary but receive a commission when your sales rise above a

specified level. In some plans the commission is paid in addition to your salary with no minimum level—or "from dollar one."

We do not recommend that a starting salesperson work on a *straight commission* arrangement. The successful straight-commission salespeople are usually those with years of experience and established customer followings in their territories, or those who represent very large companies with a built-in market demand and established sales volume for their products.

The commission system is more prevalent in the apparel industry than in textiles, and for good reason. The volume of most large textile companies is far greater than their counterparts in the apparel industry. If salespeople at these firms were offered a straight commission, many of them would become millionaires overnight!

Most companies offer their salespeople a *"draw,"* or advanced payment, against the planned commission. The draw is a sum paid weekly, bimonthly, or monthly, and it is deducted from the monthly commission. Basically the amount of the draw is calculated on the previous year's shipments or potential sales during the current year in the salesperson's territory.

For example, a salesperson may be expected to earn $30,000 in a given territory for the year. Based on this projection she may be issued a monthly advance, or draw, of $2,500. If she meets this projection she will come out "even" with the company at the end of the year.

If she exceeds her monthly draw the salesperson will then be compensated for the extra sales with additional commission. Likewise if the salesperson fails to meet the minimum commission stipulated by the draw, she will "owe" the company money. This amount will be deducted from a future commission statement, although she will be guaranteed her draw each month.

The draw system offers considerable security as compared with straight commissions, providing the salesperson with a regular income throughout the year. It is therefore the pay system most highly recommended to beginning and intermediate salespeople. In addition to giving you a fixed income the company has demonstrated a vested interest in you by agreeing to the draw and confidence in your ability to cover the draw through your salesmanship.

The third pay system, *salary-plus-commission,* also offers the advantage of a regular fixed income level throughout the year. In addition your salary is "irrevocable," and remains in your possession whether or not you meet the company's sales projections for your territory.

For example, you may receive a $200 weekly salary, plus a small commission (usually about two percent) on all sales above $5,000 each week. Or you may be paid your salary plus a commission on *all* sales transacted that week. Either way your minimum pay level remains the same, and you can only *increase* your income by your sales efforts.

CALCULATING THE COMMISSION

The usual commission in the apparel industry, in both straight commission and draw-against-commission arrangements, is six to eight percent of *net* shipments. Merchandise which you have sold but is returned by the customer, is substracted from your *gross,* or total, sales. In addition, a "trade discount" of eight percent for on-time bill payments by customers is deducted from the gross. Therefore your net pay equals the difference between your gross sales and merchandise returns and trade discounts which accrue against those sales.

For example, a salesperson generates $100,000 in merchandise shipments for the month, on which she is paid a six percent commission. About $5,000 worth of merchandise has been returned due to damages, late deliveries, shipping errors, or other common problems. In addition a trade discount of eight percent, or $7,600, is deducted from her gross sales. The commission is calculated as follows:

Gross shipments (sales)	$100,000
Less customer returns	−5,000
	95,000
Less 8% trade discount	−7,600
Net shipments (sales)	87,400
Rate of commission (6%)	×.06
Total Commission for Month	$5,244
Less monthly draw	−2,500
Amount due salesperson	$2,744

There is one additional ingredient which is part of all three of the common pay systems and should not be neglected by you in your paycheck negotiations: *expenses.* The costs of doing business are a very important variable in your final paycheck. Whether you assume these expenses, or whether they are absorbed by the company, is a piece of information you should know before accepting the job.

Selling expenses include any predetermined costs of doing your job. The most common ones are lunches, dinners, and other entertainment of buyers; gas, airfare and related transportation costs; telephone, cable, postage, and other communications charges.

While expense accounts are no longer as unrestricted as they were during the boom economy of the early 1960s, they are nevertheless important factors in determining what your final take-home pay will be. Obviously if the employer asks you to shoulder all of these costs, you will wind up with a pay envelope that is considerably thinner each month.

If you accept a salaried position, even if a commission or bonus is added, you should make sure an adequate expense account is built into your pay system. If you don't feel your basic selling expenses are being covered by the employer, tell him. It just doesn't pay to have your hard-won earnings eaten up by run-of-the-mill expenses. (Most companies automatically offer expense accounts to salaried employees.)

Likewise if you are on a draw-against-commission pay system, your draw should include adequate expense money. Generally speaking only the heartiest of salespeople—those on straight commission—pay all of their own expenses. But these well-seasoned professionals earn more than enough to cover their expense "nut."

Armed with this information you are prepared to negotiate your salary with the employer. Don't settle too easily for a pay scale you consider inferior to your abilities or less than most other companies pay. Let the employer know you're aware of the salary scales currently in use in the industry, and you are not about to be coddled into an inferior rate of pay.

Here are some key questions to ask in the course of the pay negotiations:

1. What is the company's compensation system?
2. What type of compensation system was your predecessor getting? (If there has been a change in compensation systems, why?)
3. Are all salespeople on the staff paid according to the same system?
4. What are the company's shipping figures for the previous year in the territory or list of accounts you are about to take over?
5. How many *active* accounts (those buying the company's product) are located in the region, as opposed to *inactive* accounts (those which have been dormant or unopened).

In determining your pay potential it is important to get a profile of the proposed sales territory: Is it different in size from when the previous salesperson handled it? If so, why? Is it an established, well-developed territory, or is it a new one with many undeveloped accounts?

Any way you look at it apparel-textile sales is one of the best-paying of all fields in today's job market. Make sure you are getting your fair share.

Succeeding at Sales

*Y*our success as a salesperson will depend to a large degree on your mastery of a set of rules and principles utilized by all effective salespeople. In today's competitive marketplace, the selling process has been refined to a series of objectives. Logic and organization are paramount in the achievement of sales goals.

IMAGE OF THE SALESPERSON— YESTERDAY AND TODAY

In the past the salesperson carried a pejorative image in the eyes of society. The salesman (there were few women in the field until very recently) was often seen as a wheeler-dealer—a con artist with little or no sense of responsibility toward his customers. He was thought to rely on high-pressure tactics to make a sale, and to have a get-rich-quick approach which often meant duping the client. In short he was regarded as little better than a peddler, concerned primarily with making a buck and improving his station in life.

But the image of apparel and textile salespeople has undergone a radical change over the last twenty years. During the 1950s and 1960s the industry experienced a technological transformation. A new generation of highly efficient, high-speed machinery came to dominate the textile business, and it was possible to produce fabrics and finished garments at uniform levels of quality which had only been a dream in years past.

The day of the "famous make" was nearing an end. Virtually every manufacturer had the ability to turn out fabrics and clothing at a consistent level of quality. As the business became automated in terms of fabrication and pattern-cutting, virtually every manufacturer found himself producing similar types of apparel to the other companies in his particular product category. It was no longer possible to compete on the basis of design and production quality alone.

Thus a new emphasis on salesmanship was established. With the same high-production technology available to all manufacturers, the success of a company came more and more to depend upon the talents and attributes of its sales force. During the early 1960s there was a sudden need for better salespeople and there arose an interest by management to train salespeople who could help a company meet the growing competition in the years ahead.

This was the time when the apparel and textile industry shifted from *production orientation,* or an emphasis on manufacturing capability and product quality, to *sales and marketing orientation,* with the accent placed on meeting the customer's needs by refining sales and merchandising techniques.

The makeup of top management of major companies in the industry started to reflect this change in strategy. The executive suites became populated with more sales and marketing professionals and less by people with production and financial backgrounds. The need was apparent at the highest levels of management to prepare for the new era of sales leadership.

The image of the salesperson underwent a metamorphosis. The salesperson now took center stage, and it was his or her abilities that became the most highly valued. Companies began to establish highly rewarding incentive plans to induce better-qualified individuals to go into sales. The pay scale of salespeople became the highest in the industry, with virtually unlimited earnings potential for the most qualified people. Major companies launched sales training programs and seminars to improve the skills of their sales staffs and to prepare them for newly created positions in *sales management.*

In short the role of the salesperson changed in three major ways:

1. Salespeople gained in status and experienced dramatic increases in earnings.
2. There were more frequent promotions of salespeople to high-level managerial positions, including company presidents.
3. A new emphasis on sales training and improvement of selling skills meant greater opportunity for individuals in other fields seeking to enter the sales profession.

As a result there are more college graduates at work in apparel and textile sales today than ever before. The salesperson is regarded as a business leader, a professional in his field, and an important part of his company's management team. He or she is regarded as a key profit-making source for both the manufacturer and his customers.

Salaries reflect this growth in status. A good salesperson today earns $25,000 to $35,000 a year; an exceptional sales professional can earn between $35,000 and $60,000. It is not unusual for a first-rate salesperson, with years of professional experience, to be earning $100,000 and up—more than many company presidents!

A SHARING OF RESPONSIBILITY

The salesperson of the 1980s has the ability not only to move merchandise out of the manufacturer's plant, but to build and sustain long-term working relationships with the company's customers, and therefore to ensure a profitable outlook for the future. The salesperson has a very difficult role. To be successful, she must give equal attention to the interests of her company and the needs of the customer.

The major responsibility of a salesperson, no matter what the product or service she is selling, is *to obtain orders*. However she must also serve as the eyes and ears of the company, providing feedback on developments in the marketplace. She provides vital information to the marketing, production, finance, design, and advertising departments of the company. Salespeople are in the best position to report on market trends and the developments at competitive companies. The salesperson provides invaluable aid in the development of new products and is often called upon to introduce "test lines" to her customers.

In the fast-paced technological environment of the modern textile and apparel industry, the products of today are destined for obsolescence in the future. It is therefore the duty of the salesperson to make sure her company is in tune with the needs of the marketplace.

At the same time the salesperson has an equal level of responsibility to her customers. She must call on accounts regularly, not allowing any one of them to feel neglected or underserviced. The order is not the end of the sales transaction, but rather the start of the salesperson's responsibility toward the customer. She must follow through on every order—make sure the delivery and production commitments are kept, and that the merchandise is shipped as ordered. If there are any changes in delivery plans, the customer must be informed.

Salespeople also inform their customers on changes which affect their businesses—changes in prices, new style trends, and fabric developments. The salesperson should be sufficiently knowledgeable to report to her customers on general trends in the market, and to alert them to new business opportunities. She must be able to handle customer complaints expeditiously.

THE SALES PROCESS

Salesmanship is a professional endeavor. There are certain fundamental guidelines that should be followed in order to perform successfully. In this section we outline the various steps in the selling process and recommend specific techniques which have proven successful for salespeople in the field.

Making Appointments
Making sales appointments saves time and allows you to line up more prospective business by phone during a shorter period of time than calling on each of your accounts cold. It also gives the salesperson more prestige and increases the opportunity of contacting the decision-maker at the client company.

Whether you choose to make appointments by phone or in writing, keep one important objective in mind: Always have a message. You should offer an idea that will show the customer how your product can benefit his business. Do not waste the buyer's time with vague and pointless calls or letters.

When making an appointment suggest a specific time or date, and have one or two alternatives in mind. Let the buyer know you will be brief and to the point, and that your sales presentation will not take more than a short time.

Remember: The purpose of your advance call is to make an appointment, *not* to sell your merchandise. Attempting to accomplish both at the same time will make your actual visit anticlimactic and weaken your total presentation.

Prospecting (Finding New Customers)
Statistically speaking a salesperson can expect ten to fifteen percent of her accounts each year to be lost due to a variety of factors: changes in product lines, retirement, business failures, market shrinkage, and other developments can cause a rapid diminution of what appeared at first to be a healthy account list.

For this reason prospecting for new accounts is an essential part of your sales responsibilities and must be incorporated into your plan for market coverage. An organized plan for prospecting saves time and earns money for the salesperson, while ensuring a continuity in sales volume from year to year.

In developing a list of prospects you should seek to define those customers most likely to buy your company's product. Can the product benefit the prospect? Does a want or need exist, or can a need be developed in conversation with the customer? Does the customer have the ability to pay, and is the price range within the buyer's scope?

Most important of all, does the customer have the ability to buy for his or her company? Look for the decision-makers. Don't waste time in sales presentations to assistants who may be important communication links, but who do not possess the authority to buy.

Once your initial prospect list is drawn up, there are several ways to expand its scope. Many salespeople use the "referral method" of expanding their reach in the marketplace. By speaking with existing accounts you can discover the names of other people who can use your company's product; once you have contacted these referred prospects additional sources of business can be uncovered, and so on. To do this effectively the salesperson must develop skill in getting the buyer to talk freely.

You can also expand your prospect list by visiting industry shows and exhibitions, and by following up by phone or in writing contacts you have made at these shows. There are several major trade shows in the textile and men's clothing industries, and a number of regional showplaces for women's apparel located in cities around the country.

In order to get the most out of prospecting, you should keep a sales diary which includes:

- Records of your calls on various clients and your track record of success.
- Telltale "quotes" from prospective customers, indicating how they feel about your company's merchandise and how they might best be approached in the future.
- Follow-ups on your original prospecting calls. A system for dating ahead on phone calls or personal visits can help you turn prospects into customers.

There is no better sales training course than that afforded by your own experience. Evaluate the results of your sales efforts and determine which techniques paid off for you most frequently.

Planning the Sales Presentation

Your sales effort begins the moment you arrive in the customer's office. Be and act busy. If you have to wait, spend time on your plans and paper work. Receptionists and assistants can provide you with helpful tips in approaching your client.

Don't over-wait. A fifteen- or twenty-minute wait is generally the maximum, and a buyer will respect you if you demonstrate that you have other people to see.

Very often a successful sales presentation will depend on how well you hit it off with the customer. A good first impression is vital, and therefore your appearance and poise should be well-developed sales tools. Radiate confidence, and address the prospect by name frequently.

Use the first few moments to get to know the prospect. Find out as much about him as possible, and show an interest in the prospect and his company. You'll need to know as much about him as possible to give him the benefits of your product.

Focus attention on the buyer's problems and how your merchandise can help solve those problems and boost his profits. Respect the buyer's time and avoid small talk. Try to wind up the presentation with some form of commitment from the buyer— that you will get the order or that he will review your presentation with his superiors, get back to you shortly, or visit your showroom to see more of your merchandise.

Advance planning helps ensure that your sales presentation will be well-directed and result in an order. It also increases the volume of your orders, as you plan methods for graduating the customer from small introductory orders to more substantial placements of business.

Planning also gives you an advantage over other salespeople, many of whom do not plan what to say to their customers in advance. As a result they frequently get off on the wrong track, annoy the customer by wasting his time, and miss out on opportunities for capturing business.

One way to plan your presentation is to *memorize* the key

selling points of your merchandise. This method is particularly useful to new and inexperienced salespeople who are still developing a personal methodology to selling. It allows you to give the buyer the complete story about your merchandise and to make sure you don't miss any key points.

In delivering a memorized presentation be careful not to ignore the buyer's reactions. Allow opportunities for the customer to respond to your talk, and develop various modifications to suit the customer's particular needs.

Another form of presentation is the *priority* approach, in which the salesperson verbally sketches a problem common to many buyers, or a specific problem of interest to one customer in particular. Then the salesperson offers a solution to that problem, suggesting the purchase of a certain type of merchandise.

For example, one apparel buyer may complain she does not have a colorful department in her store. A clever salesperson suggests she buy a complete assortment of the manufacturer's sportswear line, and thereby secures a large sale.

The priority presentation motivates the customer to participate in the selling process and arouses his or her willingness to act. To close the sale the salesperson must bring all the aspects of the buyer's problem together so that they result in the natural act of buying.

The priority approach also benefits the salesperson by allowing her to address the specific needs of each customer. Customers should be defined according to their *priority of needs.* For example, Customer A may have the following order of priorities:

1. Fashion
2. Service
3. Quality
4. Value

Clearly a fashion-directed approach would be the best in this instance, with some attention given to the company's service record, and only secondary interest paid to quality and value of the merchandise in the presentation.

Another client, Customer B, may size up as follows:

1. Value
2. Quality
3. Service
4. Fashion

In this instance the salesperson should emphasize the value of her company's merchandise in relation to its competitors, and the precautions the firm has taken to ensure quality control of its merchandise. Fashion and speed of delivery should be down-played, but not ignored, in this presentation.

The priority presentation is most productive for the salesperson who is a good extemporaneous speaker and expresses herself well. Professional salespeople learn how to avoid getting side-tracked on frivolous small talk and to keep the discussion focused on the merchandise.

For major sales transactions an *in-depth presentation* is often the most productive. The salesperson utilizes a survey, filmstrip, charts, or other forms of visual presentation to impress the buyer with the research and development which have gone into design and manufacturing of the product. Sometimes a salesperson will present statistics relating to the *share of market* of a particular type of clothing or the population of different consumer age groups—junior, contemporary, young men's, etc.

The in-depth presentation allows the salesperson greater time to gather and analyze facts that will help motivate a sales transaction. It allows for a more polished presentation and eliminates wasted time. However it is also more time-consuming and expensive to plan than the other methods and, therefore, is usually reserved only for major presentations to large, important customers.

Some general rules hold for any type of sales presentation. A good presentation should be simply stated in words the buyer can understand. Appeals should be both logical and emotional, and a confident and friendly atmosphere should be established at the outset. Strategy should be different for selling to a single buyer or to a group, or committee, of buyers. Every presentation should be brought to a close—not left hanging open-ended—by making the decision *easy* for the buyer.

Handling Objections

The trained salesperson recognizes certain common negative reactions by buyers and learns how to handle these routinely and effectively. Sometimes the buyer's objections are unfounded. They may be rooted in discrimination or arise from a fear of making decisions. These factors can be overcome only by inspiring confidence in yourself as a professional and developing a harmonious working relationship with the customer over a period of time.

However there are some standard objections which can be expected. For example, a buyer may indicate he needs more information about your company or about his own requirements. In this case it should be clear to the salesperson that a strong statement must be set forth on the benefits of her product line and how it fulfills the customer's needs. This sort of objection actually should be welcomed by the salesperson, since it indicates an interest in the product and is the buyer's way of asking for more details.

Another buyer may resist making a purchase because he is satisfied with his current suppliers and does not want to change. In such cases the buyer has to be convinced by the salesperson of the value of the new product and how it will repay the need for change and "sacrifice" of other merchandise in the customer's hands.

Some other common objections, for which every salesperson should be prepared, are:
- Price objections—prices too high or low for the customer's needs.
- Product objections—sometimes referring only to details of the product, other times to the entire product concept.
- Objections to the company the salesperson represents.

- Objections to acting and making a decision. (The salesperson should be alert to other underlying reasons for postponing buying.)
- Delivery problems—objections to delivery dates which are too late or too early.

Many of these objections can be effectively countered by using the "why" technique. When the objection is made, and you do not feel it is valid, the best approach can be simply to ask the question, "Why?" In many instances the customer winds up answering his own objection, and you are in a position to move on to another selling point.

No sales presentation should be so rigid that it cannot be altered once an objection is raised by the buyer. You should plan standard responses to as many of these common objections as possible *before* the presentation, so that you can handle them deftly and are not put on the spot during the meeting with the customer.

A positive mental attitude will help the salesperson defray unnecessary buyer objections. In all instances the salesperson should refrain from arguing with the buyer and remain open to objections and other forms of buyer participation. The salesperson shouldn't be so strong-willed as to rule out the buyer's complaint, which very often may provide useful information in altering the product line or the company's marketing direction.

The best salespeople pose as helpers and advisers to their customers, rather than as adversaries. Understanding the customer's objections and offering truthful responses can be the best sales tool a salesperson has at her disposal.

Closing the Sale
The "close" of any sales transaction is the most delicate part of the presentation. The buyer should exhibit confidence in making the purchase and leave in a positive state of mind, pleased with having bought your product.

Trick methods should not be used to secure a closing. Any knowledgeable buyer can recognize this form of manipulation, and an otherwise successful sales presentation can be abruptly ruined.

The best approach is to *assume that the sale is made.* When asking for the order, give the buyer a choice—which colors do you prefer, which delivery date is best, do you like the fabric range? Have a pencil and order sheet ready, and ask for information— how to ship, terms of payment, when deliveries are to be made, etc.

Once the order has been taken make sure the customer understands its benefits. Build a series of acceptances, or "yes" answers, and obtain affirmative decisions on minor points like size breakdowns, packing, hangers, etc.

There are some standard closing techniques which you can use; special situations can be communicated to the buyer in order to expedite the closing of a sale. However these techniques should be used truthfully. Misrepresentation is likely to be discovered and will not only ruin the sale but also destroy a profitable ongoing business relationship with the customer.

Here are some examples of "special situation" closings:

- *Conditional close*—"I'm already sold out, and I honestly don't know if I can take your order. I will have to check and see what provisions can be made."

- *Future event*—"Buy now, or you will pay more after September 1"; or, "There are mounting shortages of this type of yarn, and unless you buy now I can't promise you'll be able to order it later." Newspaper articles and other forms of documentation can be used to assist in this method of closing.

- *SRO (Standing Room Only)*—"We only have a limited supply left"; or "This style cannot be reordered at a later date, so you will have to order the full amount now"; or "The line is so strong, we can only offer you a certain assortment of styles."

Once you have mastered these basic sales techniques and embellished them with your own personal selling abilities, you will be on the road to successful salesmanship and a financially rewarding career in apparel and textile sales.

The Road Life— Making It on Your Own

*P*erhaps the most challenging and adventurous area of the apparel and textile sales field is territorial sales work—known in the industry as "road selling" or "outside sales." For a person seeking independence, a good deal of traveling and variety in her life, and the adventure of discovering new and formerly unknown sources of business for her company, road selling can be an exciting and rewarding alternative to selling in the company showroom.

One sales territory might be centered in a major city, covering outlying suburbs and nearby metropolitan areas. Such a territory is usually called a "key account" area, since it probably contains many of the company's largest customers, which are naturally located in the big cities.

Another territory may cover a wide expanse of rural terrain, including small and medium-sized cities scattered widely about, and encompassing many small specialty stores and small-scale department store chains. These are termed "regional territories," since they usually cover a widespread geographical region and necessitate constant travel—usually by car—on the part of the salesperson.

In this chapter you view each type of sales territory through the eyes of a woman currently involved in outside sales work. In taking a job as a road salesperson it is important to assess your own preferences and capabilities. Are you prepared for a lot of independence, moderate to heavy travel, and more than a few nights spent by yourself in hotels and motels? If so regional territory sales may be for you.

On the other hand, are you inclined to be rooted in one place —a large city, for example—while undertaking many short day trips or overnight stays to cover accounts in outlying areas? If this suits your lifestyle then key account selling may be your best choice.

Either way it is clear that opportunities for women in "outside" apparel and textile sales have never been better. Some large apparel and textile companies are actually seeking women to do this type of sales work, since they have found women to be highly effective and conscientious in developing and maintaining their account business on the road.

According to Charles Cain, president of Koret of California, a large San Francisco based manufacturer of women's sportswear and dresses, "The outlook for women in territorial sales today is excellent. If a woman wants to lead an interesting life and would like to earn a lot of money in this business, I would advise her to go on the road."

Koret is one of several apparel firms which have hired women to cover sales territories as diverse as New York City, the Washington-Philadelphia corridor, the Carolinas, Texas, and the San Francisco home-office area. These manufacturers are so interested in developing women for important sales territories, that they are willing to undertake considerable effort in training and "subsidizing" a new salesperson until she is able to support herself completely on the commissions she has earned.

At Koret, for example, new saleswomen are paid a salary to start, in addition to a percentage of their sales, until they are sufficiently skilled to go onto a straight commission basis. Cain estimates it takes most starting saleswomen about a year to develop to this level of proficiency.

The training program has proved successful both for Koret and its saleswomen. "They have developed naturally into professional salespeople," says Cain. "Our saleswoman in the San Francisco area is going to be our top salesperson for the year in California. These women are aggressive, have a good deal of self-confidence, and can work hard. It's turned out to be an interesting challenge for all of us."

Marilyn Howard is a charming, attractive, and energetic middle-aged woman. She is also an extremely talented senior sales executive with Koret of California. In a thirteen-year association with that company she has risen from a temporary "gal Friday" to a key account executive for the large New York City territory.

"Of the seventeen sales territories in the company the New York City area covers the biggest accounts in the country," she says. "I work with the buyers and merchandise managers of these large stores, and I know most of them on a very friendly basis.

"I like working a major territory," Howard says. "There's more stability here and less turnover of accounts than in the smaller cities. And I'm perfectly happy not doing a lot of traveling. Many buyers from stores in the outlying areas travel into New York to do their buying, so the need for my traveling is minimized."

Howard, who is now in a senior capacity to many salesmen within her own company, says she was readily accepted by the men in the firm once she had proved herself. "Whether you're a man or a woman, it's your ability that counts in this business. The important thing is to know what you're doing and to bring in business," she says.

Before joining Koret, Howard worked for a variety of smaller women's apparel manufacturers where she frequently found herself to be the only woman on the sales staff.

"Because the companies were small I was able to work with all the large accounts myself. There's a definite advantage to being with a small company when you're starting out in the apparel business, and then moving up to positions with larger firms later on. With a small company you learn a lot of things the average salesperson doesn't know—fabric selection, pattern-cutting, production, and shipping. You get valuable training in operations and finance, as well as sales."

Howard has kept a close eye on her earnings capacity in her rise through the ranks to her current senior sales position. "I frequently left one job for another because the money was better. Once I knew I was earning more money than the men on the force, it was a real kick for me."

"There are things I don't like about the road life—living alone, eating alone, taking care of myself on the road. But I chose this job intentionally. It gives me independence and freedom—I don't have to say 'boo' to anyone."

Speaking is Catherine Jourdan, salesperson for a Paris-based men's and women's sportswear manufacturer with offices in New York City. Jourdan's sprawling regional sales territory includes major cities like Miami, Tampa, and New Orleans, as well as the sparsely populated countryside throughout the Southeastern states of Florida, Arkansas, Oklahoma, Mississippi, and Louisiana.

"I've opened up seventy-five percent of our accounts in this region myself," says Jourdan. "The salesman who used to cover this region didn't know what he was doing. He never sent any orders to the home office in New York. I came down here and started to work in Miami, where I got $50,000 in orders on my first sales trip!"

When covering a large geographical area it is important for the salesperson to draw up a planned itinerary of account calls. The great distances between accounts necessitate planning many calls in advance and tying in prospecting calls with prearranged sales visits to existing accounts. (This technique is discussed in greater detail later on in this chapter.)

Like many of her counterparts in the road sales field Jourdan utilizes an established sales planning strategy:

1. She makes up a complete list of all existing accounts in a given city or rural area.
2. She calls each of these accounts in advance, notifying them

when she will be in their area, and lining up as many specific appointments as possible.

3. Once she has arrived in a given city, she fills in her free hours by prospecting "cold" for new accounts. "Most buyers just sit around their stores during the week and get bored," she says. "They are interested when I call on them. It gives them an opportunity to see something new and different."

4. She maintains a list of "inactive" accounts—stores which formerly bought the company's line—and "prospective" accounts which the firm has never sold, but which are major factors in their respective areas. She visits these accounts to announce new merchandising ideas and to show them some new styles which may interest them in placing new business.

5. After Jourdan has completed a sales trip she follows up by sending buyers she has visited personal invitations to see the new collection when it is introduced in the New York showroom. She also keeps them informed of new additions to the merchandise line as these occur.

"Selling on the road enables me to find out a lot about customer likes and dislikes," she says. "If a customer doesn't like an item from the line, I always ask why. And I scout around to see what's selling at the retail level wherever I go."

Jourdan and other road saleswomen find they must develop hard and fast rules for handling troublesome situations which arise during their travels. They become skilled at maintaining friendly working relationships with both male and female customers, but learn to keep these associations within businesslike bounds.

"Being on the road as much as I am, I am careful not to let men think that I need their company," Jourdan maintains. "I enjoy establishing friendly relationships with my customers. But if a guy tries overtly to 'pick me up,' I'll turn him right off."

Each saleswoman determines where she will draw the line in such instances. Some prefer to avoid dinner engagements with men who are over-friendly, while others rule out after-dinner activities such as drinking and dancing. In addition some sales-women have developed novel strategies for fending off would-be Romeos. Jourdan's solution? "I wear a wedding ring when I'm traveling, even though I am single. It avoids the discussion," she says.

Many women who take to regional selling find, after a certain period of time in the field with a single company, they can achieve even greater financial rewards and independence by representing additional manufacturers. In a sense they begin to set up their own miniature sales agencies, taking on one or two additional noncompeting merchandise lines.

Jourdan eventually plans to undertake such a multiline selling approach. "I would like to carry other merchandise in addition to sportswear—bags and accessories, for example," she says. "In this way I could sell the same buyers several different types of merchandise and take greater advantage of my traveling time and expense."

Whether you choose a geographical "road" territory or a key-account sales position in a major city, it is important to under-stand certain basic concepts of *sales territory management.* Fol-lowing are some guidelines for managing a sales territory which are recognized and utilized by regional salespeople in both textile and apparel selling.

TIME ALLOCATION AND PLANNING

It is important for a regional salesperson to evaluate the amount of time necessary to service each city or rural area in her territory. As a regional salesperson time is your most important commod-ity. Your ability to control it, and to allocate the appropriate amount of time for calling upon each account, will determine your success and earnings potential in covering the entire region.

It is important for a salesperson to organize her time schedule according to the relative importance of her accounts. Naturally she will want to devote more time to the larger customers and those who have traditionally placed substantial amounts of business with her firm. But it is also necessary to allow enough time in each sales trip for calling on smaller accounts—which added together can produce a considerable sales volume for the company—and inactive or prospective accounts, which may develop into future sources of business.

In planning your method of regional coverage consider the following key questions:

1. How many _active_ accounts are in your territory? Where are they located? Conceptualize your territory in terms of _clusters_ of active accounts—groups of customers which can be called upon in a visit to a single city or rural area.

2. Determine the _volume_ each account does with your company on an annual basis, and also which types of products each customer is likely to buy. Once this has been done the accounts should be coded as follows:

   a. _Key accounts_—the largest accounts which together contribute up to eighty percent of your territorial volume. These should be year-in, year-out customers which do business with your company on a regular basis.

   b. _Secondary accounts_—smaller accounts, some of which do not order on a regular basis, which together account for the remaining twenty percent of the volume in your territory.

   Traditionally only a handful of key accounts contribute the lion's share of volume in a given sales territory. The secondary accounts are likely to include a far greater number of customers, each contributing only a minor percentage of the overall volume for the territory. Therefore your strategy should be as follows: (1) Concentrate most of your selling time on the "a" accounts, maintaining and building these accounts to optimal sales levels; and (2) spend the balance of your time developing as many "b" accounts as possible into larger "a" accounts. It is vitally important not to neglect these smaller accounts, many of which have the potential to become major customers in the future.

These "b" accounts should be treated as a type of "insurance policy" for you. Together they can account for a substantial amount of business, and it is important to maintain a *diversified* account list, rather than keeping too large a concentration with a few major customers. There is safety in numbers, and a large account list will ensure stability and a constant sales income for you—even if one or two major accounts are lost.

3. Maintain an updated information file of buyers' names, secretaries, assistant buyers, merchandising and management officials for active accounts. Develop a similar file for inactive and prospective accounts.

4. Rehearse your typical sales presentation, and *time* it, so you can plan the amount of time you will need to spend with each account. This will help you to stay on schedule when traveling—a particularly important consideration when there is a considerable distance between account calls.

5. Determine the best means of transportation to each part of your territory. Sometimes it will pay for you to fly to a remote part of your territory and rent a car there. Even though your travel expenses will be greater, you may save valuable time in which to service additional accounts and obtain more business in a given location.

6. Plan an organized pattern for calling on the accounts in each part of your territory and for the territory as a whole. Many salespeople use a. *clover-leaf* pattern of account calls (see page 89), which enables them to cover each part of their territory efficiently and to travel the entire territory in a systematic, time-conserving manner.

For example, City A may have two large accounts and six smaller ones. The large accounts should be called upon first, followed by secondary account calls, in a predetermined sweep of the metropolitan area. Once all account calls have been completed in City A, the salesperson moves on to City B, City C, and City D, repeating the same pattern in each.

The objective of the clover-leaf approach is to facilitate complete coverage of the territory, while organizing it into segmented units, each of which can be covered in one or two days' time. The salesperson also intersperses calls on inactive and prospective accounts in each city or territorial segment.

PROCEDURES FOR ROAD SELLING

After a system of territorial coverage has been arranged, several procedures will enable you to keep track of your sales work effectively.

All appointments with key and secondary accounts should be made in advance. Never drop in on an account unannounced, a practice which is sure to result in frustrating losses of time and traveling expense. It is important that the customer knows when to expect your visit, and that you confirm as many appointments as possible before making your trip to make sure the buyer will be available as planned.

In order to keep track of appointments, it is important to own and maintain an *appointment book* in which to register the date, time, and place of each call, and the person to see at each company. Your appointment book should also be used to record the following information:

- Notations of your objectives for each sales call, and plans for following up on your visit.
- Reminders of phone calls, meetings, and other details which must be attended to on your trip.
- Travel and entertainment expenses. These are usually tax deductible, and it is important to have a written record of all expenses for tax purposes.

We recommend a monthly appointment book such as the "Pocket Day-Timer," with suitable space for recording all of the above-listed information. One tip: You need not order binders or other expensive paraphernalia often sold with these books. The paperback refills will suffice and are available for under $10 in most stationery stores.

Appointment records should be kept on a daily basis. If allowed to accumulate at the end of the week or month, this paperwork will rapidly develop into an uncontrollable and chaotic situation.

In addition to the appointment book every salesperson should maintain a _card file_ containing the vital information about each account—both for active accounts, and inactives or prospects. A file box containing 3″ by 5″ index cards is the handiest. Each card should include the following facts: company name, address, and names of contacts for each account; phone number; account history; best time of day or week to call, and other pertinent data.

Some salespeople file their index cards alphabetically for the entire territory. However we recommend that you subdivide your cards according to your predetermined territorial _segments_ and maintain an alphabetical listing for each. In this way your cards will be automatically grouped according to travel sequence and easy to use in planning your road calls.

You are likely to modify this filing system based on your first-hand experience in covering the territory. In all cases records should be simple and easy to use, whether you are in your office or car.

In addition to the appointment book and card files, it is important to maintain a record of orders placed with the home office and copies of shipment invoices which you receive confirming deliveries of merchandise. Orders should be filed alphabetically, and shipping information should correspond with the original orders. The easiest way is to attach a copy of the shipping invoice to the order and file both in alphabetical order.

Planning and recordkeeping are the prerequisites for successfully managing a sales territory. With these organizational aids a salesperson becomes in a real sense a "manager," supervising her company's relationships with all of the accounts in her territory

—from account calling to final shipping. It is this sense of full control which makes territory management a rewarding pursuit for the thousands of men and women who earn their living "on the road."

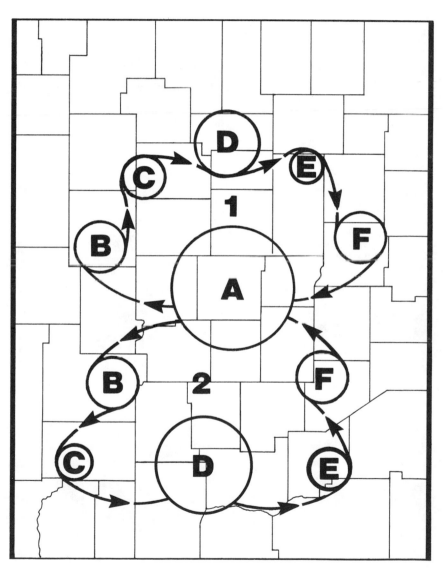

Clover-Leaf Pattern of Account Calls

Coping—How to Deal Practically with On-the-Job Pressures

*T*his book would be neither complete nor accurate if we were to ignore the realities of on-the-job pressures and the need to deal in a productive manner with the frustrations, setbacks, and emotional crises confronting any woman or man in today's competitive job market.

The key to success in apparel and textile sales, as well as in many other fields, may be seen as a combination of both *offensive* and *defensive* techniques. By "offensive," we mean those tools of selling and management which enable a salesperson to perform well and to gain recognition within her company. The sales strategies, methods, and personal characteristics described in the previous chapters are all part of the offensive effort to build sales volume and increase the market acceptance of the company's products.

However a professional sales executive cannot afford to overlook the importance of caution and circumspection in her dealings with superiors and fellow salespeople. It is important to assume a "defensive" strategy when confronted with hostility or unfair competition from other individuals who are seeking to advance their careers at the expense of one's own.

Because the involvement of women in apparel and textile sales is a recent development, some resistance from male peers is to be expected. The outstanding salesman almost always evokes a feeling of jealousy in his fellow staff members. But the exceptional saleswoman often presents a dual problem for salesmen on the staff, threatening not only their egos but also their sense of virility and self-respect.

Difficulties may also be encountered in relationships with superiors and customers, who feel threatened by an aggressive saleswoman. Sometimes the hostility breaks out into the open, as in one instance we know of where a customer actually requested that he deal with a salesman, rather than a woman.

We cannot tell you how to handle every situation which arises in the interactions of a salesperson with her fellow staff members. You will, without doubt, learn your own personal techniques for maneuvering in the tricky waters of intra-company politics and for fending off encroachments on your sales responsibilities by competitors within your own company.

However we can report with certainty that, having interviewed several women in top sales and management positions, the most successful women have developed systems for coping with "people problems" which occur in their dealings with peers, superiors, or customers.

The first step in *coping,* or learning to live within a competitive sales environment, is to *recognize* the problems that exist. Ignoring a source of confrontation, or pretending that it does not exist, is the best way to ensure a continuation and even an escalation of the problem.

The second step is to *counter* the source of aggression and to develop a strategy for overcoming it, rather than becoming mired in an ugly confrontation. Each woman must develop a system for dealing confidently and in a controlled manner with interpersonal problems as they arise.

The third and most difficult stage in the art of coping is *anticipating* problems before they occur. Certainly, at the start of any sales job, a cautious attitude toward other salespeople in the company is to be recommended, especially with those men who exhibit "sexist" attitudes.

Most professional saleswomen establish ground rules in their relationships with men on the job which help avoid problems. For example:

  • A saleswoman should refuse any offers by fellow staffers to pick up the tab at lunch or dinner. This practice clearly reduces the woman to the role of a "date," rather than regarding her as an equal in business.

- Romantic involvements with other men in the company, whether they be peers or superiors, should be avoided. There is no easier way for a man to deflate a woman's image than to show the other guys that he has won her over romantically and therefore removed her as a competitor.
- Entanglements with male customers are also risky. Word travels fast, and pretty soon the salesmen are reporting to the manager that the woman is succeeding for reasons other than her sales ability.

A CASE STUDY IN "COPING"

Most of the saleswomen we talked to have experienced problems at one time or another in their relations with other women and men on the job. Some managed to work these problems out, to overcome the resistance by other employees to their successful selling. Their status and level of responsibility in their respective companies rose accordingly.

However more than a few women have stumbled over thorny interpersonal predicaments. Agitated by the problems they encountered these women allowed themselves to get emotionally overwrought, resulting in a lower level of job performance and sometimes in prolonged depression.

Mary S. is the sales manager for a division of a large textile company. She is one of the few people in her field who holds a Masters in Business Administration, and she succeeded in being promoted rapidly from a sales trainee to sales manager in just a few years. (Her company has been advancing a few women to key management positions as part of an affirmative-action program.)

As sales manager she is responsible for directing an all-male sales force and reports to a male senior executive. In an interview she candidly discussed problems she has experienced with men in her company and her effort to cope with them:

"I feel underpaid in comparison with male sales managers in the company. I complained about this to my boss, but he only offered me a stock option in the company to keep me quiet. If I were a man I'd be paid about twice what I'm getting now. I'm still not happy about it.

"When I first started to work as a salesperson I was the only one on the staff without an account list. They knew I had the ability to sell—I had proved myself as a trainee—but they were afraid to give me the actual responsibility. It wasn't until a salesman left that I was given an actual list of accounts to work on, rather than hand-me-downs from the other salesmen.

"Sales meetings are very often held informally—in the men's room. Since, as a woman, I had no access to that area, I missed out on some important meetings and had to work double-time to catch up.

"My rapid advancement was due to the fact that I not only increased the size of my orders, but also built the company's distribution and added many important accounts for them. Nevertheless there was at least one key account which was denied me because the client refused to deal with a woman. This was a source of great frustration to me, since I had already proved I could handle the business.

"I get readings from men all the time. I can tell at a first meeting if the customer is looking at me in a certain way, that he has something in mind other than business. Some men will touch me while they talk to me, and this is a clear danger signal.

"I'm the only woman in my department. All of the salesmen on my staff are younger and less educated than I, but more experienced in the field. I've just had a few years of selling experience, and yet I'm their boss. Sometimes I think they resent the hell out of me.

"I feel as if I'm fighting every inch of the way. My position would be difficult enough for a man. But because I'm a woman, I haven't been given the authority I need over these men to accomplish my objectives. I feel that I am constantly being se-cond-guessed by management and unable to win the full respect of my staff."

A PROGNOSIS FOR SUCCESS

The above illustration of a female sales executive under pressure is intended to give you an awareness of the realistic, on-the-job problems which face many women, yet are rarely discussed in the literature on selling.

However it is our contention that you need not become mired in problems of the type that afflicted Mary S. Careful attentive-ness to the demands placed upon you by other people, together with the requisite job experience, will help you to successfully cope with interpersonal problems, and sometimes actually turn these problems to your advantage.

According to Dr. Helene J. Newman, a psychologist specializ-ing in the problems which affect working women, the case of Mary S. illustrates a woman succumbing to interpersonal prob-lems largely because she lacks necessary experience and a positive approach to her job.

"Women who have been most successful in business have very few problems relating to men," Newman says. "The important thing for a woman is to utilize her work skills to their fullest and by so doing, win the respect of the other workers—both men and women."

Newman maintains there is danger in a woman's gaining too much responsibility too fast. The growth in corporate affirmative-action programs under the Equal Opportunity Act (see Chapter Four) has resulted in some women being over-promoted beyond their level of ability.

"A lot of women feel they deserve a top spot just because they are women," she notes. "Women who are handed a plum job for this reason often start out on the defensive, since they really do not feel they have the necessary skills to perform the work effectively.

"However if a woman has the proper background—and has taken the time to acquire job skills through a variety of employment experiences—she will find herself much more secure and less susceptible to staff rivalries and competition."

Newman adds, "A lot of women who have risen too quickly just *because* they are women feel inadequate. Rather than blaming themselves for their inexperience, they *project* their insecurities onto other people, creating interpersonal and even sexual problems which really don't exist at all."

In the case study given above, Newman points to the fact that Mary S. has developed insecurities because of her lack of experience compared to the salesmen in her department. Mary S. interprets problems with customers and subordinates as sex-related, when actually these problems may be symptoms of her own inexperience and lack of important job talents.

"A skilled manager will take the time to understand her problems thoroughly," Newman says. "If Mary S. had talked to the members of her sales staff on an individual basis, she probably would have found that each one had his own problems, and that these were not necessarily related to her ability to manage.

"For example, one salesman may have felt the need to graduate to a more important sales territory. Another may have felt underpaid, or slighted, by receiving an inadequate bonus. Mary S. could have sorted out these problems in discussions with her salesmen and coped with each one effectively, rather than interpreting them together as sexual biases."

If management is reluctant to give a woman a salary and title commensurate with her ability, says Newman, the best strategy is to give the job a "test run" to demonstrate her ability to her superiors. "A woman can tell her boss that for a year she will accept an inferior salary, but that in the course of the year she will demonstrate her value to the company, and by so doing *earn* her salary increase," Newman says. "In this manner she will gain the respect of management because she will be paid as a result of her performance—not simply because she is a woman. And she will alleviate her anger and be able to focus more clearly on the job at hand."

How does a woman cope with exclusive male groups? Newman has a simple solution: "A woman can call a meeting of her peer group and tell them frankly that she resents being excluded from important meetings. She should make a direct bid to be part of the situation."

Envy by subordinates is another problem which can be deftly handled by the experienced female sales executive, and sometimes even turned to her own advantage. Newman advises the woman to "encourage envious people on her staff to emulate her. She should tell them that once they have achieved the proper level of experience, they will be able to take her job, or a similar management position, within the company. There is no mystique here. Responsibility and status in the company are the direct results of hard work, and the staff should be made to recognize this fact."

A direct approach also should be taken with superiors who question a woman's seriousness about pursuing a career in sales and management. "If the woman tells her boss directly that she is interested in a long-term association with the company and does not plan to abandon the job for family reasons, management will respect her attitude."

Once a woman has achieved a feeling of well-earned confidence in her job, Newman says, she should not be afraid to *act herself.* "It's all right to be feminine as long as you have the job skills to back it up," she says. "There's nothing wrong with wearing a stylish outfit, and there's no reason to fear touching another person as a means of self-expression. The better prepared you are, the more comfortable you will feel behaving as a woman."

Family Management—The Working Mother's Challenge

*T*oday's female sales executive has enormous responsibility. She must compete daily with men and other women for the advancement of her career objectives and the success of her company. Her ability to manage her sales territory will result in millions of dollars of volume for her company, and through her accomplishments the company will either grow and prosper, or weaken and lose its importance in the marketplace.

She is constantly undergoing scrutiny by management—sales managers, corporate vice-presidents, and the company's chief executive officer—all of whom are motivating her toward greater productivity. For, as every salesperson knows, her success is largely dependent upon her ability to beat her previous year's sales record, and to attain an ever-increasing amount of business for her company.

The female sales executive who is also a mother has an even more difficult role. In addition to mastering all of the challenges of her job she is called upon to fulfill the equally demanding role of parent. In spite of a trying job schedule, which may include heavy travel and a great deal of physical as well as mental strain, she must find time to devote care and attention to the upbringing of her children and the maintenance of a home life.

At first glance this dual responsibility of the sales executive who is also a mother appears staggering. How to juggle all the commitments of work—late-night meetings, days on the road, business lunches, and dinners—with the responsibilities of the home life? Are there enough hours in the day to function effectively on the job and to also meet the tasks of family life?

More and more women are finding that they *can* gain complete fulfillment by nurturing their careers and their families at the same time. They have developed systems for successful *family management* which allow them to spend adequate time with their spouses and children, and to realize the joys of motherhood as well as the exhiliration of a promising career.

Several interviews with women in sales who are also mothers reveal three important criteria of successful family management: (1) Time apportionment, (2) dividing of responsibilities with spouse, and (3) employing full or part-time housekeeping help.

TIME APPORTIONMENT

A sales executive will spend a minimum of forty hours a week on the job. This time is inflexible, and there is virtually no way of cutting back on working time that will not jeopardize the position and career of a salesperson.

In most cases the working day will be completely absorbed by the responsibilities of the job. Of crucial importance is the midday lunch period, when a considerable amount of business is transacted with major accounts over lunch, or when important office meetings are called over sandwiches.

Therefore it is during the evenings and on weekends or holidays that the working mother plans her family time. Her schedule is not without sacrifice. Leisure time normally devoted to social and recreational activities—dinner parties, bridge, outings, etc., by a full-time homemaker—is given over to the needs of family and household requirements. In fact even with the time requirements of the office there are more hours available in the average week for time spent with the family than there are working hours.

As many working mothers will tell you, family time is not necessarily an extension of work time. After the rigors of the working world, family time can be a peaceful, welcome respite. And just because work takes so much time away from the home, these hours with children and husband become all the more precious and valuable as a time to build close family bonds.

According to Gloria Gelfand, sales executive for a major women's apparel company, "My children are given my 'quality time.' I have never performed the typical roles of a suburban social hostess. I forewent a lot of the social amenities I felt were unimportant—the parties, dinner engagements, clubs—to concentrate on what was important to me in my personal life.

"I have found that I am able to cram into a weekend as much time with my children as most mothers fit into a full week. When I am with my family during this time, there is nothing else in my life. Evenings and weekends are strictly 'family times.' "

Gelfand says the most difficult and trying period was when her children were very young. "I had to decide whether to sacrifice my work or my social life. Since my career was very important to me, I decided to take the time from my social and leisure activities."

When her children were infants Gelfand consulted a pediatrician and arranged a schedule which would allow her to spend as much time as possible with them. "The children took late-day naps—from about four to six o'clock—and then, when I came home, we woke them up and all had dinner together. I was able to spend every evening with them."

Although Gelfand and other working sales executives/mothers are not typical, they are clearly developing a new concept of family management which allows them to mesh their job commitments with the needs of their families. As more and more women embark on sales and other business and professional careers, it is likely that the traditional image of woman-as-housekeeper will be considerably modified. As women give more attention to career goals, they will continue to develop new and effective techniques for managing family time—rather than being governed by it.

THE ROLE OF THE SPOUSE _____

The realities of working motherhood place a new responsibility on the husband. Just as the mother's role is reworked and modified to allow for her career, the husband must adjust his role in the family to accommodate the career objectives of both spouses as well as the needs of children.

The husband must be prepared to assume a broader range of responsibilities and duties in the maintenance of the household. A good deal of the physical labor involved in housework—maintenance of the home, shopping, errand-running—must be shared by the husband. In a home where both spouses are working, the husband cannot afford the luxury of delegating housekeeping duties to his wife.

The maintenance of a family time schedule also requires that the husband sacrifice some of his free time. If his wife is detained at the office, he must be prepared to fill in. In fact husband and wife can develop a symbiotic relationship concerning household and family. Each must be prepared to cook, clean, and care for the children in the absence of the other.

Of course developing a family lifestyle which offers room for both spouses to pursue their independent careers is sure to involve some painful adjustments. According to Gelfand, "The first real crisis usually develops when the baby is sick. Who's going to stay home and take the baby to the doctor?

"What you need is an understanding with your husband whereby you ask each other, 'Who's got the roughest day today?' If your workday is not expendable, then your husband must be prepared to step in."

Gelfand notes, "I knew that whenever a situation like this arose, I could count on my husband. In that sense I was very, very lucky to have such a wonderful, understanding spouse."

The time has come for men to reevaluate their role in the family. With women also serving as family "providers," it is only natural that men exhibit a commitment to sharing housework on an equitable basis with their wives.

HIRING A HOUSEKEEPER

Virtually any mother who has taken on a full-time career will attest to the importance of a capable, conscientious housekeeper. Even when both spouses attempt to devote a large share of their leisure time to the care and welfare of the children, there are still those long daytime periods during which the presence and attention of an older, caring person is vital.

Particularly in the case of young children and babies, it is necessary to have an attentive adult present during the day, from the time when both spouses leave for work until they return late in the day or early evening. A qualified housekeeper is, in many cases, the key ingredient in maintaining a healthy family environment while both parents are away at work.

Unfortunately, with a growing number of mature women entering the work force, the demand for trained housekeeping help has grown out of proportion to the number of housekeepers available for employment. Labor Department statistics show that out of about 25,600,000 women with children aged seventeen or under, almost 11.5 million, or forty-six percent, are already in the labor force. And this figure keeps growing. At the same time there is a noticeable decline in the number of women or men available for full-time or part-time housekeeping work.

The most common procedure for attracting housekeeping help is to place an ad in a local newspaper describing in detail the work involved and the salary. In addition many communities have employment agencies which specialize in placing domestic help. However you should be cautioned against expecting immediate results. Some agencies report they have as many as sixty or seventy requests for every housekeeper available for employment, and the competition is keen for well-qualified housekeepers with experience and excellent personal characteristics.

If you cannot locate a suitable person either through an ad or by contacting the agencies, you can place a request on file with your local state employment agency for a minimum of thirty days. You will be required to place a simultaneous newspaper ad referring applicants directly to the state agency.

If, after undertaking all these procedures, you have not been able to engage a housekeeper, you can file a labor certification indicating that you are willing to employ a specific person from a foreign country. This is a delicate task, and you may require the aid of an attorney who is knowledgeable of immigration laws. You should also note that the federal government has placed greater restrictions on hiring alien workers due to the current high unemployment rate, and you will probably need to present a well-documented case for "sponsoring" an alien worker.

Aside from the scarcity of domestic help, hiring a housekeeper —especially full-time—is an expensive proposition. Average wages of full-time housekeepers are about $125 a week, not including related expenses such as carfare and living costs if the housekeeper is "living in."

However there are tax advantages which help defray part of the expense. According to a recent amendment of the tax law, tax-payers receive a credit, rather than a deduction, for child-care expenses if both parents are employed full-time or part-time, and if their children are under fifteen years of age. The credit—which is actually a dollar-for-dollar reduction in your final income tax bill —amounts to twenty percent of child-care expenses up to $2,000, including housekeeping expenses, per child. For a family of four, the tax credit would equal $400 per child, or $800. (In applying for such a tax credit the parent with the lower salary must show that he or she earns as much as the domestic worker, or the credit is reduced proportionately.)

Many working mothers are finding a more economical solution to the child-care problem in community day-care centers. These centers provide daytime care to children of individuals living in their respective communities and are run either by professionals or on a rotating basis by the mothers themselves.

You may want to investigate whether such day-care centers exist in your community and, if so, whether they suit the needs of your family.

Opportunities in Management—Woman Power Development

*M*anagement of a sales territory is excellent training for sales management positions in the apparel and textile industry. If a salesperson can effectively and profitably manage her own sales territory, there is an excellent chance that she can develop into a successful sales manager, with responsibility for an entire sales force.

If a salesperson has developed all of the techniques for running a successful territory—time budgeting, account building, prospecting, and the maintenance of a profitable account list—then she is in a good position to guide other, less experienced salespeople in the management of their territories.

The transition from selling to sales management is, in fact, not a difficult one for most people. The characteristics of a good salesperson—attention to details, following through on prospects and sales calls, being aggressive yet truthful in dealings with customers and one's own corporate management—are essential qualities of successful sales managers.

As we discussed earlier, the contemporary salesperson is not just an order-taker, but a well-disciplined business manager in her own right, whose chief objectives are to earn profits for her company and her customers. As such she often finds herself an excellent candidate for promotion to a sales management position within her own company, or elsewhere in the industry.

Sales management involves management of people—the sales staff of an apparel or textile company—to achieve the sales and profit goals of the company. The sales manager must harness the abilities of other people to accomplish the corporate objectives of her firm. She must learn to work through other people to accomplish the sales goals for the company.

BRIDGING INTO A SALES MANAGEMENT POST____

Graduating into a management position is, to a large extent, the result of your ability to communicate your desire to become a manager to the top executives in your firm. Aspiring managers have many opportunities to communicate these feelings with their superiors on a day-to-day basis.

For example, meetings with your sales manager provide an excellent forum in which to discuss your future with the company. The important factor to emphasize in these meetings is not your own self-fulfillment, but how you feel you can benefit the company over the long run.

Exhibit control and self-motivation in your daily sales responsibilities. It is important for management to perceive you as a sales executive in full control of your territory. By exhibiting your command of your own sales assignments, you are communicating to management your eligibility for a managerial position involving control of many sales territories and the individual salespeople who cover each.

Most importantly, when a management position opens up in your company and you feel you are qualified for it, *apply for it.* Ask to be considered for the position, rather than waiting for management to contact you. Very often a promising salesperson misses an opportunity to enter sales management simply because she fails to put in for the job.

If there are no opportunities for assuming a management post within your own company, you should keep an eye out for openings in sales management at other companies. You can usually spot these through classified ads in trade newspapers, by contacting employment agencies in the field, or by word of mouth from your friends and associates in the industry. Sometimes a customer can provide you with an excellent lead to a job opening with another manufacturing company.

MANAGING PEOPLE PROBLEMS

You will find in your rise through the ranks of the apparel and textile sales field that your success will often depend on how well you get along with other people. Especially important is your ability to cope with "people problems"—the range of interpersonal conflicts arising from the competitive nature of the business.

Most common among the sources of people problems facing professional sales managers are: (1) Internal competition from salespeople on one's own staff, (2) resentment of superior sales performance, (3) insecurities of other people who feel threatened or injured by the success of another person in their department, and (4) relating to one's own superiors.

In many cases it is best to overlook these attitudes and to find a means of cooperating with the troublesome person, in spite of the obstacles they present to your own success. Calling attention to the problem often exacerbates the conflict and allows the hostile person to become an even more disruptive influence on your career.

However in certain cases it is necessary to have a plan for handling interpersonal problems. As a woman in sales, you can expect a certain amount of resistance from men in your company, both from management and peers on the sales staff. Although women are now entering the field in greater numbers than ever before, it is surprising how some men still cling to the old all-male image of the sales force.

The following case studies demonstrate some of the problems you are likely to encounter in your progress through the ranks of the apparel-textile sales field, along with some suggestions for handling them.

"End Run Around the Boss"

Joan is a sales manager with a well-known textile company. While her superior, the vice president is away on business, she is instructed to report directly to the president of the company.

Joan seizes the opportunity to cement her relationship with top management. In the absence of the vice-president she attempts to deal with the company president on both a business and social level. She and her husband invite the president and his wife to dinner and play tennis with them on the weekend. In the office Joan directs all of her sales reports to the president himself.

It doesn't take long for the vice-president to notice Joan's new approach. He discovers that he is being bypassed in the reporting process, and that Joan—one of his key executives—is no longer responsive to his instructions.

Consequently the vice-president accuses Joan of insubordination and asks the president for her dismissal. The president, who at last feels abused by Joan's aggressiveness, consents, and Joan loses her job.

Joan's strategy in going around her superior ultimately backfired, leaving her without a job. Her mistake, though serious, is a common one, and in a sense she was lured into it by the periodic absence of her superior and the need to report directly to the company president when the vice president was away.

To avoid the "end run around the boss" problem, it is important to maintain an appropriate attitude of respect and attentiveness to one's immediate superior, and to support his or her policies. In contacts with top management, the sales executive should speak highly of her own direct superior and exhibit respect for this person.

The "Kid Gloves" Problem

Shortly after taking a sales position with a small textile company, Laura finds she is being given special attention and consideration by management. As the only woman on the sales staff she is not subjected to the hard criticism frequently directed by the sales manager to her male counterparts on the staff. Rather Laura is called aside privately by the manager and "encouraged" in a gentle manner to improve upon her shortcomings.

Laura's account list consists of many small but secure customers, none of which presents a difficult challenge. When a big prospect is assigned it is given to one of the men on the force. Likewise when a tough problem arises with a major account, a salesman is always asked to clear it up.

While Laura's position looks comfortable from the outside, it will grow increasingly difficult for her to function effectively with this company and to earn the respect of her peers and managers. She is being "shielded" from the difficult decisions and tough problems of the sales business, thus losing valuable experience. By assuming only small, safe accounts, she is being denied the important experience of working with major customers; the profit potential which such large accounts provide for company and salesperson alike, and the opportunity to gain advances through merit.

As a woman in sales it is important to be treated as a businessperson—not as a woman. The saleswoman must make it clear to her superiors that she does not want or expect special consideration.

Even on small, seemingly insignificant matters, it is important for a woman to preserve her businesslike approach. For example, when taking a buyer for lunch—male or female—it is customary for the salesperson to pay the bill. When going to lunch with a salesman in the company it should be strictly "Dutch treat." It is important not to allow the fellow salesman to take on a superior, condescending attitude. You must be regarded at all times as a full-fledged member of the sales team.

Keeping Subordinates in Line
Barbara, who has spent five years as a salesperson for a men's sportswear company, is promoted to sales manager in charge of a twelve-person sales staff. Although she is prepared for some resistance from her former peers, and deftly manages to earn their respect in most areas, one salesman presents a more difficult situation.

Harry, a salesman with the company for over twenty years, is a self-avowed "male chauvinist," and frequently passes disparaging comments about women in business. Up to now Barbara has managed to avoid Harry's comments by staying out of earshot. Now, as his superior, she senses his resentment growing and becomes extremely upset by his loud comments at sales meetings and group lunches. After a while she can no longer tolerate his attitude and suddenly calls him into her office to announce that he has been terminated.

But by "firing" Harry, Barbara has only increased the resentment of the other salespeople toward her. They now view her as a callous, hard-skinned tyrant and have become increasingly hostile toward her.

Barbara's error was in not attempting to earn Harry's respect for her sales expertise. She passed up many occasions to demonstrate her ability by helping Harry solve particular problems with his accounts. By turning against him, rather than working with him to earn his respect, Barbara lost an experienced salesman and seriously damaged her rapport with the rest of the staff.

When working with a dissident or problematic staff member, the professional manager should try to win that person over to her side by whatever means possible. Very often frequent counseling sessions with the dissident staff member will result in a new-found rapport or common goal which transcends the initial conflict. Exploiting the conflict can only result in damage to the manager's career, and detract from the harmonious operation of the sales department.

THE CHALLENGE

As a people-oriented profession apparel and textile sales places great demands on its practitioners to get along with others. Solving business problems is not enough to guarantee a successful career in this field. The added ingredient of understanding other people and being able to work harmoniously with them to attain a common goal for the company is a primary factor in determining the success of each individual salesperson.

In dealing effectively with other people and overcoming the many obstacles they present each business day, the salesperson emerges as a leader not only in her company but in the sales field as a whole.

Bibliography

Aspley, John Cameron. *Sales Manager's Handbook*. Chicago, Illinois: Coleridge Press, 1964.

Bird, Caroline. *Born Female*, rev. ed. New York: David McKay Co., Inc., 1974.

_____. *Everything a Woman Needs to Know to Get Paid What She's Worth*. New York: David McKay Co., Inc., 1973.

Blumenthal, Lassor A. *Great Sales by Today's Great Salesmen*, paperback. New York: Macmillan, Inc., 1966.

Boucher, Francois. *20,000 Years of Fashions*. New York: Harry N. Abrams, Inc., 1967.

Burton, Gabrielle. *I'm Running Away from Home, But I'm Not Allowed to Cross the Street*. (Available from KNOW, P.O. Box 86031, Pittsburgh, Pennsylvania, 15221.)

Calasibetta, Dr. Charlotte. *Fairchild's Dictionary of Fashion*. New York: Fairchild Publications, 1975.

Djeddah, Eli. *Moving Up: How to Get High Salaried Jobs*. Berkeley, California: Ten Speed Press, 1978.

Dual Careers. Manpower Research Monograph #21. Washington, D.C.: Government Printing Office.

Farrell, Warren. *The Liberated Man*, paperback. New York: Bantam Books, Inc., 1975.

Fasteau, Marc Feigen. *The Male Machine*. New York: McGraw-Hill, Inc., 1974.

Feinberg, Samuel. *Management's Challenge: The People Problem*. New York: Fairchild Publications, 1976.

Friedan, Betty. *The Feminine Mystique,* 2nd ed. New York: W. W. Norton & Co., Inc., 1974.

Gellerman, Saul W. *Motivation and Productivity.* American Management Association, 1963.

Gold, Annalee. *How to Sell Fashion,* 2nd ed. New York: Fairchild Publications, 1978.

_____. *75 Years of Fashion.* New York: Fairchild Publications, 1975.

Guide to Federal Laws Prohibiting Sex Discrimination, A. Clearinghouse Publications #46. Washington, D.C.: Government Printing Office.

Hampton, Robert E., and James Barton Zabin. *College Salesmanship.* New York: McGraw-Hill, Inc., 1970.

Janeway, Elizabeth. *Between Myth & Morning: Women Awakening.* New York: William Morrow & Co., Inc. 1974.

_____. *Man's World, Woman's Place: A Study in Social Mythology.* New York: William Morrow & Co., Inc., 1971.

Jarnow, Jeannette A., and Beatrice Judelle. *Inside the Fashion Business.* New York: John Wiley & Sons, Inc., 1968.

Johnson, and Dunn. *Managing the Sales Force.* General Learning Press, 1973.

Jones M., and J. Healey, editors. *Miracle Sales Guide,* student ed. New Jersey: Prentice-Hall, Inc., 1973.

Joseph, Marjory L. *Introductory Textile Science,* 2nd ed. New York: Holt, Rinehart & Winston, Inc., 1972.

Keyes, Ruth A., and Ronald A. Cushman. *Essentials of Retailing.* New York: Fairchild Publications, 1977.

Ley, Sandra. *Fashion for Everyone.* New York: Charles Scribner's Sons, 1975.

Man-Made Fiber Fact Book. (Available from Man-Made Fiber Producers Association, 1150 17th Street, N.W., Washington, D.C. 20036.)

Payne, Richard A. *How to Get A Better Job Quicker.* New York: Taplinger Publishing Co., Inc., 1972.

Pederson, Carlton A., and Milburn Wright. *Selling: Principles and Methods,* 6th ed. Homewood, Illinois: Richard D. Irwin, Inc., 1976.

Peter, Dr. Laurence J., and Raymond Hull. *The Peter Principle.* New York: Bantam Books, Inc., 1970

Pizzuto, Joseph J. *Fabric Science,* revised by Arthur Price, Allen C. Cohen. New York: Fairchild Publications, 1974.

Pogrebin, Letty Cotton. *Getting Yours: How to Make the System Work for the Working Woman.* New York: David McKay Co., Inc., 1975.

Private Employment Agencies Directory. (Available from National Employment Association, 2000 K Street, N.W., Washington, D.C. 20009.)

Roth, Charles B. *Secrets of Closing Sales,* 4th ed. New Jersey: Prentice-Hall, Inc., 1970.

Shapiro, Steven. *Supervision: An Introduction to Business Management.* New York: Fairchild Publications, 1978.

Stanton, William J., and Richard H. Buskirk. *Management of the Sales Force,* rev. ed. Homewood, Illinois: Richard D. Irwin, Inc., 1974.

Whitney, Rubin, Thomas Hubin, and John D. Murphy. *The New Psychology of Persuasion and Motivation in Sales.* New Jersey: Prentice-Hall, Inc., 1975.

Wingate, Dr. Isabel B. *Fairchild's Dictionary of Textiles,* 6th ed. New York: Fairchild Publications, 1979.

_____. *Textile Fabrics and Their Selection,* 7th ed. New Jersey: Prentice-Hall, Inc., 1975.

Women's Role in Contemporary Society. The Report of the New York City Commission on Human Rights. September 21–25, 1970, paperback. New York: Avon Books, 1972.

Working Woman's Guide to Her Job Rights, A. Women's Bureau Leaflet #55. Washington, D.C.: Government Printing Office.

MAGAZINES AND TRADE PAPERS

American Fabrics Magazine. Doric Publishing Co., Inc., 24 East 38th Street, New York City, 10016 (quarterly).

American Textiles Reporter Bulletin. 106 Stone Avenue, P.O. Box 88, Greenville, South Carolina 29602 (monthly).

Daily News Record. Fairchild Publications, 7 East 12th Street, New York City 10003.

Knitting Times. 51 Madison Avenue, New York City, 10016.

Modern Textiles. Rayon Publishing Corporation, 303 Fifth Avenue, New York City 10016.

Textile Chemist and Colorist, Journal of the AATCC. P.O. Box 12215, Research Triangle Park, North Carolina 27709 (monthly).

Women's Wear Daily. Fairchild Publications, 7 East 12th Street, New York City 10003.

Index